CARLYLE AND THE SAINT-SIMONIANS

The Concept of Historical Periodicity

Carlyle and the Saint-Simonians

The Concept of Historical Periodicity

BY

HILL SHINE

1971

OCTAGON BOOKS

New York

Reprinted 1971
by special arrangement with The Johns Hopkins Press

OCTAGON BOOKS
A Division of Farrar, Straus & Giroux, Inc.
19 Union Square West
New York, N. Y. 10003

Library of Congress Catalog Card Number: 71-120666

ISBN 0-374-97360-1

Printed in U.S.A. by
NOBLE OFFSET PRINTERS, INC.
NEW YORK 3, N. Y.

TO

MY MOTHER

CLAUDIA PEARSALL SHINE

FOREWORD

The idea that Carlyle was influenced by Saint-Simonian thought is about a century old. Most of the critics who have held the idea have based it upon the similarities in social philosophy. Early among those who commented on the influence was the French socialist Antoine Dilmans. Near the middle of the Nineteenth Century he suggested that Carlyle's thought was fundamentally Saint-Simonian.[1] And since Dilmans' time, the relation to the Saint-Simonians has been noted a number of times. But the way for a definitive study of influence was not opened until the century had changed. Not until 1903 did Eugène d'Eichthal, son of Carlyle's Saint-Simonian friend Gustave d'Eichthal, publish the important correspondence between Carlyle and the Saint-Simonians.[2] Still no definitive study appeared. In the second decade of the new century, the now celebrated critic Louis Cazamian could do little more than allude to the "influence diffuse et vague de Saint-Simon" upon Carlyle's optimism.[3] The third decade furnished estimates that were at least more positive. They came from French, British, and American writers. Bouglé and Halévy considered Carlyle a conscious dis-

[1] A. C. Taylor, *Carlyle et la pensée latine* (*Études de littérature étrangère et comparée*, 8: Paris, Boivin, 1937), pp. 51-55.

[2] "Carlyle et la Saint-Simonisme," *Revue historique*, LXXXII (1903), 292-306. Three of these four letters from Carlyle to Gustave d'Eichthal were later printed in English in "Carlyle's Letters to the Socialists of 1830," *The New Quarterly*, II (London, 1909), 277-288.

[3] Louis Cazamian, *Carlyle* (*Les Grands Écrivains Étrangers*) (Paris, Bloud et Cie, 1913), p. 119.

ciple of Saint-Simon.[4] D. A. Wilson believed Saint-Simon's *Nouveau Christianisme* was " a stimulant to the expansion of *Sartor*." [5] And Professor Neff went so far as to say that the contents of *Sartor* were "almost entirely a synthesis of the ideas of the German philosophers and the Saint-Simonians." He further believed the Saint-Simonian social gospel was " a clarifier of many ideas which had been struggling for expression in his [Carlyle's] own mind." [6] The fourth decade produced three notable discussions of the subject by American scholars. The first of these three latter-day discussions, which was by Professor Cofer, dealt with only the social philosophy. And Cofer, like Halévy, pronounced Carlyle a disciple of Saint-Simon.[7] The second discussion, which was by Professor Ella M. Murphy, differed diametrically from Professor Cofer's conclusions. That is, she was unable to find convincing evidence of Saint-Simonian influence upon Carlyle's thought.[8] The third

[4] *Doctrine de Saint-Simon,* Exposé, première année, 1829 (edited by C. Bouglé and Elie Halévy, Paris, 1924), pp. 64-65. See also Halévy's *History of the English People* (English translation, London, 1927), III, 161. Original French edition, 1912.

[5] *Carlyle to " The French Revolution "* (London, 1924), p. 190.

[6] Emery Neff, *Carlyle and Mill. An Introduction to Victorian Thought* (second revised edition, New York, Columbia University Press, 1926), pp. 217 and 215 respectively. For Professor Neff's full treatment of Carlyle and the Saint-Simonians, see pp. 209-221. Unfortunately Neff in his documentation makes only three page-references to works published by the Saint-Simonian Society. This treatment in *Carlyle and Mill* is more detailed than the treatment in the same scholar's later *Thomas Carlyle* (New York, 1932).

[7] D. B. Cofer, *Saint-Simonism in the Radicalism of Thomas Carlyle* (College Station, Texas, 1931), p. 30. Though Cofer quotes or digests some fifteen letters from Carlyle and six works by Saint-Simon himself, he does not show control of the important writings of the Saint-Simonian Society.

[8] Ella M. Murphy, " Carlyle and the Saint-Simonians," *Studies in Philology,* XXXIII (January, 1936), 93-118. Miss Murphy's article is especially valuable in giving information about the personal contact and

and latest discussion of Carlyle's connection with the Saint-Simonians occurs in Mrs. Louise Merwin Young's recent book, *Thomas Carlyle and the Art of History*.[9] Unlike the writers already named, Mrs. Young stresses the contribution of the Saint-Simonians to Carlyle's philosophy of history. Her conclusions on this point, though she does not substantiate them by proofs, are remarkably close to the conclusions that will be stated in the present study.[10] She incisively points to the prin-

correspondence between Carlye and the Saint-Simonian Society and in its able analysis of the essay " Signs of the Times " and several of the writings of Saint-Simon. But, presumably she lacks first-hand contact with many of the publications of the Saint-Simonian Society, and she fails to see Carlyle's indebtedness for his concept of historical periodicity. And there are some other short-comings. For example, she does not use the references to the Saint-Simonians in *Two Note Books of Thomas Carlyle* (ed. C. E. Norton, Grolier Club, New York, 1898), pp. 113, 183, 193, 198, 201, 205, 248. The first of those references (*Two Note Books*, p. 113) shows that Carlyle first heard of the Saint-Simonions in April or May of 1827, thus correcting Miss Murphy's belief (*S. P.*, XXXIII, 104) that Carlyle's first knowledge of the Saint-Simonians dates from 1830. (The same passage in *Two Note Books* corrects Gerhart von Schulze-Gaevernitz's date of 1824. See *Thomas Carlyle, Seine Welt- und Gesellschaftsanschauung* [second ed., Halle, 1897], pp. 29-30). She says Carlyle translated Saint-Simon's *Nouveau Christianisme* late in 1831. Actually the translation was made late in 1830 (see *The Letters of Thomas Carlyle, 1826-1836* [ed. Norton, London, 1889], p. 178). She also confuses—as one might easily do—two collections of Carlyle's correspondence: that is, she refers several times to *Early Letters* when she should refer to *Letters* (see *S. P.*, XXXIII, 105, 106, 108). Her confusing Alexander Carlyle, the late nephew of Carlyle, with Alexander the brother (*S. P.*, XXXIII, 118) is another easily understandable error.

[9] Philadelphia, University of Pennsylvania Press, 1939, pp. 67-68, 198. Unfortunately Mrs. Young's treatment of the Saint-Simonian influence is very brief. It occupies one paragraph in the text of her book and one note at the end. And even so brief an account is not free from a striking error: she states (p. 198) that Carlyle corresponded with Saint-Simon himself in 1830. This error in fact is probably the result of dependence upon secondary sources of information about Saint-Simon and the Saint-Simonians. (Her only references to sources [p. 198] are to Carlyle's *Two Note Books*, p. 158, and to Flint's *Philosophy of History in France and Germany* [London, 1874] pp. 164-165).

[10] The present study had been in process several years and had been

ciple of historical periodicity as an important relation
between Carlyle and the Saint-Simonians. She realizes
that historical periodicity is " one of the fundamental
premises on which Carlyle erects his philosophy of history. . . . The idea proved extremely fruitful in Carlyle's
analysis of social change, and he anticipates modern
sociological tendencies in his use of it." [11] Furthermore
she knows that Carlyle's acceptance of a theory of
periodicity did not begin with the year 1830, when he
first came into contact with the publications of the
Saint-Simonian Society. " Long before this Carlyle had
accepted a theory of periodicity, but the close parallels
between his expression of the idea and that of the St.
Simonians suggest that he used their elaboration in
detail." [12] In spite of the fact that her brief comment
hardly more than touches upon the store of evidence,
a better three-sentence summary statement than Mrs.
Young's of the relation between Carlyle and the Saint-
Simonians would be very difficult to produce.

In summarizing those studies, one feels that the whole
problem of Carlyle's relation with the Saint-Simonians
needs re-examination. No detailed or definitive study
of all the aspects of the problem or even of all the
primary material exists. The only detailed studies—
Professor Cofer's and Professor Murphy's—both stress
the social or the political aspect of the problem. Both
of these studies fall far short of completeness with respect to the Saint-Simonian publications; they disagree
diametrically in their conclusions; and they ignore the

---

written in rough draft before Mrs. Young's study appeared. Only this
introductory section has been altered by her discussion of Carlyle's relation to the Saint-Simonians. Her book, if inadequate on the present topic,
is in many other respects admirable.

   [11] *Thomas Carlyle and the Art of History*, pp. 67-68.
   [12] *Ibid.*, p. 198. On p. 68 she says that Carlyle borrowed from Saint-
Simon " the systematic elaboration of the principle."

question of historical periodicity. The most recent discussion—Mrs. Young's—unlike the others, stresses historical periodicity. But her study is, more than the other two, incomplete, in that it makes only the slightest attempt to examine and document the sources.

Our present study, though adequate in primary material, is, alas, incomplete in the other respect. That is, leaving the social aspect of the relation for later treatment, the present study deals with Carlyle's indebtedness to the Saint-Simonians for his mature concept of historical periodicity. As it proceeds, it will, nevertheless, show how his mature social viewpoint is undergirded and made intelligible by the theory of historical periodicity. By thus tracing Carlyle's most fundamental relation with the Saint-Simonian Society, this study (it is hoped) will throw some new light on the entry of a too-little-known element in Nineteenth Century English thought.

It is pleasant to express here my gratitude to the following. To President Ralph Waldo Lloyd of Maryville College, who from funds of which he has charge has met the expenses of procuring microfilm from Paris [13] and has provided me substantial aid in meeting expenses of this and of an earlier publication on Carlyle. To the librarians and their assistants at the University of North Carolina, Duke University, and Maryville College, who have long given me use of the resources of their libraries. To Yale University Library and its officials—especially Mr. Bernhard Knollenberg, Mr. J. T. Babb, and Miss Emily Hall—for permission to study and quote from valuable unpublished Carlyle manuscripts. To Helen Chadwick Shine, who first showed

[13] Much of the material published by the Saint-Simonian Society has been microphotographed in Paris and is now in the possession of Maryville College Library.

me the use of microphotography, without which this study would have been impossible. To Miss Clemmie J. Henry and Miss Della Mae Allen of Maryville, who are responsible for preparing this and other tedious manuscripts for me. To Professor Ralph Stokes Collins of Maryville, who has read this study carefully enough to point out and eliminate some mistakes. To the members of the University of Tennessee Philological Club, who have listened to me patiently and criticized helpfully. And most of all, to Professor John Manning Booker of the University of North Carolina, who, during the nearly twenty years that he has taught me in his incomparable way, has shown me many things. He had much to do with my undertaking the present study; during the intermediate stages of work, contact with his mind did more than any other to keep me moving; and in the final stage, he read the manuscript critically.—To him and them all, my thanks.

TABLE OF CONTENTS

———

CHAPTER I

CARLYLE'S EARLY CONCEPT OF HISTORICAL PERIODICITY
(BEFORE MID-1830)

I

In order to discover the part that the Saint-Simonian influence played in Carlyle's mature concept of historical periodicity, the first step is to ascertain the extent to which periodicity appeared in Carlyle's writings before he had read the Saint-Simonian publications. His writings before August 1830 certainly do reveal a concept of historical periodicity.[1] But that concept was one that changed as he changed, and that grew as he groped for fuller comprehension. In relation to the writings up to the spring of 1829, perhaps instead of *concept*, one should use the term *fragmentary glimpses of a concept*, which, when drawn together within a paragraph, look somewhat like what he later came to hold as a philosophy of history.

Let us gather the glimpses and far-off preparations one by one and draw them together. In the working out of his own moral philosophy of life Carlyle had early come—as many other romantics had come—to distrust negation, denial, and lack of faith.[2] Though this atti-

---

[1] The term *historical periodicity* means that human history shows, not a constantly straightforward progressive development, but a periodic alternation of (1) eras of advance and (2) eras of recession. After an epoch of advance, regularly comes an epoch of recession; then advance again, then recession; and so on. Later, Carlyle was to distinguish *epochs of advance* as *epochs of faith*, and *epochs of recession* as *epochs of denial or disbelief*.

[2] "State of German Literature," *Critical and Miscellaneous Essays*

1

tude does not yet appear important in the present investigation, its significance will gradually emerge. For this attitude was eventually to undergo fusion with the notion of epochs of belief and epochs of unbelief, as Goethe called them, or organic and critical epochs, as the Saint-Simonians called them. Faith and belief, in Carlyle's mind during the middle 1820's, had become connected with the faculty reason, as distinguished from the faculty understanding,[3] and a pseudo-Kantian distinction between reason and understanding had rationalized for him the notion of continuity in change.[4] This notion, which was part of the idea of progress common in Carlyle's early writings and in the writings of his contemporaries, was to be symbolized later, when it was mature, in the phoenix-figure in *Sartor Resartus*. By November 25, 1827, he had noticed Werner's application of the phoenix-figure to the changes in that very changeable romantic's religious faith.[5] But, without aid of the phoenix-figure, Carlyle was familiar with the notion that spirit—which he later called Divine Idea, after Fichte [5a]—reappears in various ages under various forms. Specifically, it reappears under various forms of poetry [6] and of religion.[7] Furthermore, in Carlyle's

(Centenary edition, London, Chapman and Hall, 1899), I, 41 and 85-86. This essay was finished by October 19, 1827.

[3] Entries for December 7-18, 1826, in *Two Note Books of Thomas Carlyle*, p. 83.

[4] Compare *ibid.*, p. 4 (March 25-26, 1822) with p. 83.

[5] *Essays*, I, 144.

[5a] The view that the manifestations of the Divine Idea change in various ages is common in Fichte's *Über das Wesen des Gelehrten* (see J. G. Fichte's *Sämmtliche Werke* [ed. J. H. Fichte, Leipzig, 1845], VI, 352, 366, 406, 415, 438, 446). Carlyle knew this popular work of Fichte's by August 1827 (see my "Carlyle and the German Philosophy Problem during the Year 1826-1827," *PMLA*, L [1935], 818).

[6] March, 1826, "Goethe," prefixed to Carlyle's translation of *Meisters Wanderjahre*. See *Wilhelm Meister's Apprenticeship and Travels* (Centenary edition of Carlyle's *Works*, London, Chapman and Hall, 1899), I, 28-29.

[7] By November 25, 1827, "Werner," *Essays*, I, 143.

thought during 1828, various forms of those reappearances or manifestations were already correlated with certain general attitudes of mind in different ages. That is, he considered belief characteristic of Milton's era.[8] He considered unbelief characteristic of Voltaire's later era.[9] And again he considered belief characteristic, at least to some extent, of the present age in Germany.[10] Early in 1829, he noted development stages, but not periodicity, in the history of philosophy.[11] He even guessed at recurrent cycles or periods in the development of individual minds, and wondered if that kind of periodicity was parallel to seasonal periodicity in nature.[12] But thus far he had discussed belief and unbelief, continuity and change, and the process of development through different forms, chiefly in terms of German psychology and German philosophy.

In the essay on Voltaire, early 1829, Carlyle was especially interested in the attitudes of belief and unbelief with respect to Christianity in Eighteenth Century France. He again took Voltaire as representative of his age.[13] He believed the Philosophes were criticizers, denying and destroying; though not yet affirming, they were opening the way for a new affirmation.[14] He characterized Voltaire's era in some of the same terms he was later to use in characterizing critical or skeptical epochs.[15] He was aware of a resemblance between Vol-

---

[8] By September 16, 1828, " Burns," *ibid.*, I, 313.

[9] By end of May, 1828, " Goethe," *ibid.*, I, 215-216.

[10] By end of May, 1828, *ibid.*, I, 217, 210, 208.

[11] January, 1829, " Novalis," *ibid.*, II, 38.

[12] February, 1829, *Two Note Books*, p. 132. When on this page of the notebook Carlyle uses the words *history of the world,* he apparently means merely the record of external nature through the changing seasons of the year.

[13] By March 31, 1829, " Voltaire," *Essays,* I, 401-402, 415-416.

[14] *Ibid.*, I, 465, 415-416, 459.

[15] *Ibid.*, I, 415-416, 465.

taire's age and the Roman Empire.[16] And he believed
Voltaire's age was to be superseded by an era of opposite outlook in religion.[17] But all those points are dealt
with as events and are interpreted by means of his old
moral philosophy of life that distrusted negation;[18] by
his religious meliorism;[19] or by his version of German
philosophy.[20] The points are not tied together as one
pattern of a greater historical tendency interpretable by
a philosophy of history, as he later saw them to be. He
seems simply not yet to have worked out a concept of
organic and critical epochs of history accordingly as
they characterized themselves affirmatively or skeptically toward all general beliefs or fundamental schemata. He had not worked out his later phoenix doctrine
of transition between periods. Nor had he worked out,
either, the periodic alternation of those eras, their necessary recurrence, their specific institutions, and their
dates, as parts of a great historic process. But in the
essay on Voltaire obviously he was groping toward some
such concept.

In " Signs of the Times," finished by August 5, 1829,
he made considerable advance toward the philosophy of
history that he later used. " Signs " insists that Ideas
shape practice:[21] that the Crusades, the Reformation,
the English Revolution, and the French Revolution all
followed Ideas.[22] But in his discussion of Idea he drives
his distinction between dynamic and mechanic.[23] And
that distinction seems based on the old pseudo-German
distinction between reason and understanding.[24] In
saying that the French Revolution and other move-

---

[16] *Ibid.*, I, 460-461.
[17] *Ibid.*, I, 402.
[18] *Ibid.*, I, 459.
[19] *Ibid.*, I, 460-461.
[20] *Ibid.*, I, 457-458.
[21] *Ibid.*, II, 66.
[22] *Ibid.*, II, 71.
[23] *Ibid.*, II, 68-73 especially.
[24] *Ibid.*, II, 63-64, 68. Cf. also the entry in *Two Note Books*, p. 142, written late in 1829.

ments and crises in history followed Ideas, he had not
yet clearly seen Idea as the schema or theorem of the
universe, which in certain eras is acceptible and har-
monizes all thought and action, and which—because it
only approximates truth—proves increasingly unsatis-
factory to later times. In " Signs " he does not discuss
the phenomenon of a worn-out universal schema, which
must be demolished to make way for a new. He does
grope nearer to it when he says that other ages have
been mechanistic and that mechanism has been a common refuge of weakness and discontent.[25] He even says
that discontent is promising, that the process of thinking is increased thereby, and that man must struggle
forward in it, not backward.[26] But one may ask the
Carlyle of 1829, Forward to what? The mechanic-
dynamic division of eras does not furnish an answer.
Carlyle's nearest approach, in this essay, to an answer—
but not yet the complete answer—appears on the last
page of " Signs."

There is a deep-lying struggle in the whole fabric of society;
a boundless grinding collision of the New with the Old.
The French Revolution, as is now visible enough, was not
the parent of this mighty movement, but its offspring.
Those two hostile influences, which always exist in human
things, and on the constant intercommunion of which de-
pends their health and safety, had lain in separate masses,
accumulating through generations, and France was the
scene of their fiercest explosion; but the final issue was not
unfolded in that country: nay, it is not yet anywhere unfolded. Political freedom is hitherto the object of these
efforts; but they will not and cannot stop there. It is
towards a higher freedom than mere freedom from oppres-
sion by his fellow-mortal, that man dimly aims. Of this
higher, heavenly freedom, which is ' man's reasonable service,' all his noble institutions, his faithful endeavours and
loftiest attainments, are but the body, and more and more
approximated emblem.[27]

[25] *Essays*, II, 80.   [26] *Ibid.*   [27] *Ibid.*, II, 82.

This passage comes the nearest thus far to Carlyle's later notion that man must struggle on toward a new institution, schema, or theorem of the universe that will interpret phenomena without glaring fraud.

Sometime later (late summer or early fall, 1829) in his notebook, he made a pointed comment on worn-out and deserted institutions, or schemata.

An Institution (a Law of any kind) may become a *deserted* edifice; the walls standing, no life going on within, but that of bats, owls and unclean creatures. It will then be pulled down if it stand interrupting any *thoroughfare*: if it do not so stand, people may leave it alone till a grove of natural wood grow round it, and no eye but that of the adventurous antiquarian may know of its existence, such a tangle of *brush* is to be struggled thro' before it can be come at and viewed.[28]

In that passage, as in the one at the end of " Signs," he is attempting to deal with the problem of development in history, which, on its way toward new orders, may destroy old institutions or leave them behind. But as yet he lacks, not glimpses into difficult phases of the problem, but an orderly and inclusive solution and statement of the whole historic process.

The problem became more acute as he entertained various projects of writing on historical subjects. Late in the summer of 1829 he was seriously considering Luther as a subject.[29] Soon after, he seems to have considered writing some work based upon a historical view of early periods of English literature.[30] But in October that project was overthrown by proposals for

[28] *Two Note Books*, p. 141.
[29] Before August 5th: *Two Note Books*, pp. 136-140; *Letters of Thomas Carlyle, 1826-1836*, p. 149; *Two Note Books*, p. 142.
[30] *Ibid., pp.* 143, 146-147. *Selection from the Correspondence of the Late Macvey Napier*, Esq. (ed. by his son Macvey Napier, London, Macmillan, 1879, pp. 77-78 (January 27, 1830).

a history of German literature, which became a definite engagement in late fall and early winter.[31] By January 26th, he was having difficulty in working out a basic plan for the German literary history and particularly in interpreting the Reformation Era of Luther.[32] And on March 1st, he complained that the history would nowise fashion itself into shape.[33]

On the same day (March 1, 1830) Carlyle stated his belief that a deeper view of the world was about to arise in him. He now felt that, having got rid of materialism as a result of his German studies, he was about to put aside his preoccupation with German philosophy, morals, and aesthetics, valuable as they had been, and turn to a broader interpretation, a fuller ground-plan of the universe.

I have now almost done with the Germans. Having seized their opinions, I must turn me to inquire *how* true are they? That truth is in them, no lover of Truth will doubt: but how much? And after all, one needs an intellectual Scheme (or ground plan of the Universe) drawn with one's own instruments.[34]

In short, while turning from individual aspects of the burden of the mystery, to the social and historical aspects, he had found some inadequacy in his earlier views, and felt that he must develop a concept that was more adequate.

By April 12th he had finished his speculation " On History," which he had intended to serve as the intro-

---

[31] *Correspondence between Goethe and Carlyle* (ed. by C. E. Norton, London, 1887), p. 159 (November 3rd); *Letters of Thomas Carlyle, 1826-1836*, pp. 151 and 157; *Early Letters of Jane Welsh Carlyle* (ed. D. G. Ritchie, London, 1889), pp. 154-155 (December 21st) and pp. 161-162 (January 26th).

[32] *Early Letters of Jane Welsh Carlyle*, pp. 163-164.

[33] *Two Note Books*, p. 147.

[34] *Ibid.*, pp. 150-151. See pp. 147-152 for the context.

duction to his history of German literature. For some reason, however, he was dissatisfied with the speculation, thought it would not serve its purposes as introduction, and eliminated it, before he proceeded with his writing of the main text.[35] The part thus eliminated but later published as the essay " On History " included two points that are pertinent now in his historical speculations concerning the ground-plan of the universe. The essay insisted upon the organic nature of life. Coming history, he believed, lies already shaped and inevitable in the past; the future and the past complete the meanings of each other.[36] That is, not only did Carlyle see the history of man as an organism, but he was groping toward the laws that governed the organism. And he insisted that a written history of poetry should search out and delineate the successive steps by which man had obtained the revelations of the Spirit of Nature in art and in religion.[37]

And in further work on his history of German literature, Carlyle did arrive at some notion of the manner in which the law of historical development had revealed itself in seven centuries of German literary history. Though the historical treatise itself was never finished and was never published as a continuous history,[38] his plans for the arrangement of the material involved are

[35] *Ibid.*, p. 154.   [36] *Essays*, II, 83.   [37] *Ibid.*, II, 94.
[38] The unpublished manuscript of the completed part, some ninety pages, was offered for sale by Sotheby on June 14, 1932 (Sotheby and Company, *Catalogue of Printed Books, Autograph Letters, Literary Manuscripts, Oil Paintings, Drawings and Engravings, Works of Art, China, Furniture, etc., Formerly the Property of Thomas Carlyle, 1795-1881, and now Sold by Order of the Executors of His Nephew, Alexander Carlyle* [London, 1932], p. 33, item 185. Attribution of the manuscript to 1829 is a mistake; it really dates from 1830.) Parts of the material were later reworked for the essay on Taylor's *Historic Survey of German Poetry* and for the essay entitled " Early German Literature." Those essays will be discussed later in this study.

discussed in three of his letters during the months from March to May.[39] The plan there described can be condensed as follows. The seven centuries from the Twelfth to the Nineteenth were to be treated as a succession of periods. And two of these periods show an alternation of epochs. Carlyle calls those alternating epochs *poetic periods* and *didactic periods*. The first poetic era included the *Nibelungenlied* and the Minnesingers. Characterized by the chivalric spirit, it was a poetic age, though a simple one. In it, man was for the first time inspired by an infinite idea. The succeeding epoch, a didactic one, included such authors and pieces as Hugo von Trimberg, *Reineke Fuchs*, and Brandt. It continued until didacticism reached a poetic degree in Luther. This second poetic epoch is represented by Luther and Hutten. After Luther, there came a second didactic epoch. This second didactic epoch sank into theological disputation and superficial refinement. It proceeded through Thomasius and Gottsched, down to utter unbelief and sensualism, when poetry became impossible. Then, after a transition under such men as Lessing, who was an earnest skeptic standing between two periods, came the third poetic epoch, under Schiller and Goethe. Carlyle's own words to Goethe will best describe this third poetic epoch, the beginning of a new period.

. . . under you [Goethe] and Schiller, I should say, a Third grand Period had evolved itself, as yet fairly developed in no other Literature, but full of the richest prospects for all: namely, a period of new Spirituality and Belief; in the midst of old Doubt and Denial; as it were, a new revelation of Nature, and the Freedom and Infinitude of Man, wherein

---

[39] *Correspondence between Goethe and Carlyle*, pp. 171-172 (March 20, 1830); *ibid.*, pp. 187-192 (May 23); *Letters of Thomas Carlyle, 1826-1836*, p. 164 (May 1).

Reverence is again rendered compatible with Knowledge,[39a] and Art and Religion are one. This is the Era which chiefly concerns us in England. . . . How I am to bring it out will require all consideration.[40]

That division of seven centuries into five alternate poetic and didactic epochs—comprising two full periods and the beginning phase of a third period—was the plan that Carlyle outlined in his letters of early 1830. How far he could have applied it, continues to be a question, for the work remained a fragment.[41]

Of the *History of German Literature* itself, only the first volume seems to have survived.[42] Lacking some twenty pages, which were taken out and re-worked for publication in the form of essays, the unpublished Volume I still exists, in the Manuscript Vault at Yale University Library. This work shows some approximations to Carlyle's later notion of progressive periodic mutation. Perhaps the closest are the following passages.

. . . Conviction is the parent of Action. . . . Thus new Truths may be called the most important of events. . . .[43]

[And] Literature may be called the earliest and noblest

[39a] Cf. a passage in F. Schlegel's *Lectures on the History of Literature, Ancient and Modern* (tr. H. G. Bohn, London, 1896, p. 380), which insists that a reunion of Faith and Science is [1812] about to take place.

[40] *Correspondence between Goethe and Carlyle*, pp. 190-191 (May 23, 1830).

[41] *Ibid.*, p. 209, which says that by August 31, 1830, he had written a volume and a half of the projected four volumes, and had thus come down in his narrative as far as to the Reformation.

[42] Volume I was finished late in May or early in June 1830. On May 1st (*Letters of Thomas Carlyle, 1826-1836*, p. 164), Carlyle told his brother it would be finished in a fortnight: i. e., by mid-May. And on June 8th (*Two Note Books*, p. 156), he says: "Am about beginning the Second Volume of that Germ. Lit. Hist.: dreadfully lazy to start."

[43] Thomas Carlyle's unpublished autograph manuscript entitled *History of German Literature* (Manuscript Vault of Yale University Library), p. 3.

product of man's spiritual nature. . . . From the time of the Sibylline Verses to that of the London Gazettes, the spoken or written Word, . . . prophetic, poetic, didactic, has ever been the grand index and agent of our progress. . . . [44]

The first task of a historian of a national literature should therefore be " to decipher and pourtray the spiritual form of the nation, at each successive period. . . ." [45]

But the deciphering and portraying of the spiritual form of the nation at each successive period might seem to presuppose the ability of a historian to arrive at what Carlyle calls " genetical schemes." [46]   And in that tendency of philosophers and historians to interpret history by means of genetical schemes lies, Carlyle thinks, great danger. But we cannot now examine his statements on that point.[47]

Nowhere in the *History of German Literature* does Carlyle characterize either such alternate epochs of belief and unbelief or such alternate organic and critical epochs as constitute a period in his later writings. Rather, as will be seen in a later paragraph, he seems to stress an analogy between national culture and individual culture: that is, culturally both nations and individuals pass through the phases of childhood, youth, and manhood.

Nevertheless, several times in the unpublished volume he alludes to the transition between successive eras. In the dark forests of Tacitus's Germans, says Carlyle, there

[44] *Ibid.*, p. 5.
[45] *Ibid.*, p. 9.
[46] *Ibid.*
[47] *Ibid.*, pp. 9-11, where Carlyle gives a sane discussion of " genetical schemes," three of them in particular: the attempts to account for poetry as a function of national wealth, a function of political freedom, and a function of primitive language.

already dwelt the future regenerators of Europe, under whom the old corrupt world was to be swept away as an abomination, and a new world under fairer omens for mankind to evolve itself.[48]   The ancient world [he says] divides itself from the modern by a dim chaos; over which no highway leads; only we know that in its deep, troublous, ever-fluctuating bosom the latter had its birth, the former its grave; that in this boundless anarchy, old things passed away, all things became new.[49]

The era of the Northern Immigrations

was a boundless ' shaking of the nations '; the New and the Old, the luxuriously Corrupt and the barbarously Rude, with all the elements of new worth in the one, and the fragments or traditions of old worth in the other. . . .[50]

Indeed, in a comment on the art of his own time, he even uses the Phoenix figure to suggest the method of transition that he finds imminent.

To the perfection and purifying of Literature, of Poetry, Art, all eyes are turned; for in these times the deepest interests of men seem to be involved in it; the ashes and fast-burning fragments of the whole Past lie there, from which, amid clouds and whirlwinds, the Phoenix Future is struggling to unfold itself.[51]

And a few pages later he suggests also the organic-filaments notion of growth and change that he was to use in *Sartor*. On all hands, he says, it begins to be understood that German literature

is not only a clear melodious Echo of the present Time, but also a Prophecy of a new and better Time, traces and incipient form of which already lie revealed there.[52]

It is especially important to realize that, already by mid-1830, Carlyle had used the Phoenix figure to sug-

[48] *Ibid.*, pp. 15-16.
[49] *Ibid.*, p. 22.
[50] *Ibid.*, p. 20.

[51] *Ibid.*, p. 9.
[52] *Ibid.*, p. 12.

gest the method of transition between successive eras. This seems to be his first independent use, as part of his own thought, of Werner's Phoenix figure, which he was to elaborate fully a year later, in *Sartor Resartus*.

In the description of specific past eras, the manuscript *History of German Literature*, extending through the Swabian Era, makes only shadowy contrast between classical and medieval cultures. A passage involving that contrast has already been quoted at the beginning of the preceding paragraph. But there the allusions to what Carlyle calls the ancient world and the modern world are incidental to his description of the Miltonic-Lucretian chaos of boundless anarchy that separates the two.[53] Elsewhere, when he comments more directly, his chief stress is naturally placed upon the Middle Ages. The Northern Immigrations, he says, " form an epoch in the History of the world; they are properly the beginning of European Culture; and in importance of result, perhaps second only to the appearance of Christianity itself." [54] The continuation of this passage, as quoted in the preceding paragraph, concerns the " boundless ' shaking of the nations ' " which resulted from the clash between the luxuriously corrupt old culture and the barbarously rude new one. In that clash of cultures, he adds, the weaker was obliterated; through the justice and mercy of God, the abominations were swept away. And in the new time, Christianity was to wed the Chivalry of the North.[54]

Properly speaking, from the period of the great Immigrations, at any rate from the time of Charlemagne, there was no dark age: for all Europe was learning, was at school; all hearts were animated by that noble zeal for knowledge, that unwearied seeking after it, which is in itself the best fruit and proof of Culture. . . . [55]

[53] *Ibid.,* p. 22. [54] *Ibid.,* p. 20. [55] *Ibid.,* p. 97.

Under Charlemagne,

'the discordant seeds of things' now lay in final contact and solution; and, like fair fruits, the Arts, the Power, the Moral Character of new Europe were to spring from them.[56]

Europe again saw itself spontaneously or forcibly united; not into one community, but into a kind of aggregate; "wherein dim rudiments of a common interest were becoming visible." [56] One of the deep common interests was the Christian religion; and in it, with its cloistered calm and its peace and good will, the union was complete. Charlemagne, seeing also the political or social wants of the time, fostered schools and arts too. Such a sign " betokens a new era." [56]

Among the first decisive products of this new time, we must reckon the establishment of Chivalry; a singular institution, which . . . comes forth embodied in a practical shape, in the latter half of the eleventh century.[57]

From France, Chivalry spread over the Christian world, " and for several ages represented under its customs and practices whatever was highest in the spirit of Europe." [57] Before the end of the Twelfth Century, Chivalry had arrived at its golden age. In all ranks, it became the household principle, and the private and public law. All life was colored by it.[58] In chivalry,

for the first time, the grand principles of order, of subjection to rule, were universally inculcated, and the maintenance of them made a habit and a sacred duty.[59]

And in the knightly orders, especially during the time of the crusades, " men learn[ed] to act in large combination. . . ." [59] Chivalry

[56] *Ibid.*, pp. 89-90.
[57] *Ibid.*, p. 90.

[58] *Ibid.*, pp. 90-91.
[59] *Ibid.*, p. 91.

was a translation into Practice of whatever was noblest in the Sentiment of mankind. . . .[60] Here [in the era of the crusades] at last were old German Valour and Christian Humility harmoniously blended; and the new European man stood forth at all points a Man. . . . Chivalry once more set up an Ideal Excellence in practical forms; once more brought the light from Heaven to shine on our earthly path.[60]

It was a recognition of the infinite celestial nature of Virtue, of moral Beauty; and was a devotion of life and faculty to its service.[60]

The moral philosophy of the twelfth century might put that of the eighteenth to shame; for the one knew and practically asserted, what the other had well nigh forgotten, that beyond the sphere of Sense there is an Invisible Kingdom in man, whence and not from Sense are the issues of spiritual life for him. . . .[60]

And the true ideal represented by knighthood remains, says Carlyle, to some extent a true ideal for his own time.

It was the first fair coherent figure and representation of Manhood for these modern ages; of such Manhood as modern circumstances shape out and admit for us; and though a young simple figure, yet also not without the vigour, the completeness, and graceful bloom of youth.[61]

For, in Chivalry, " man's being, the heavenly and the earthly element in it rightly adjusted, was in unison with itself. . . . "[61] Thus Carlyle elaborately discusses the Middle Ages in Europe. In that age he points out two main organizing principles, Christianity and Chivalry, and suggests that because of the harmonious union of those two great directive principles man could then find his own life full, purposive, and satisfactory. The blend of Christianity and Chivalry constituted the

[60] *Ibid.,* p. 92.   [61] *Ibid.,* p. 93.

private and public law; and all life was coordinated, colored, and elevated by it. However, it should be noted that chivalry, as Carlyle here discusses it, is more of a morality or an ethic than it is a polity.

Thereupon, having pointed out in the Middle Ages the directive principles that gave man a sense of harmony between the real and the ideal in his life, Carlyle proceeds to trace the results of man's inward harmony as it manifested itself in poetry: " soon, as indeed it ever does, that inward harmony expressed itself in the outward harmony of Poetry, of Song." [61] From Provence, in the Twelfth Century, came the soft tone of poetry. And " the ' joyful science ' [of poetry] spread abroad as rapidly as Chivalry, from which it sprang, had done. . . . " [61] Europe now became, if not a commonwealth, one great confederation; and the sympathy of parts has ever since displayed itself. Under the Hohenstaufen Emperors in Twelfth Century Germany, as elsewhere, " the spirit of Chivalry had married itself to Song. . . . " [62] In that era,

Suddenly, as at some sunrise, the whole Earth had grown vocal and musical. . . . It was a universal noise of Song; as if the Spring of Manhood had arrived. . . . This was the *Swabian Era*; justly reckoned . . . properly the First Era of German literature.[63]

To indicate the rich unity in medieval life and religion and art, Carlyle draws upon Tieck,—draws the figure of a uniting religion sheltering the people as the protective dome of a church would do. The figure is one that Carlyle later used repeatedly. In the Swabian Era, says Carlyle in words that he assigns to Tieck,

' as the pillars and dome of the Church encircled the flock, so did Religion, as the Highest, encircle Poetry and Reality;

[62] *Ibid.*, p. 98.   [63] *Ibid.*, p. 101.

and all hearts, in equal love, humbled themselves before her.' [64]

The Swabian Era was the

Youth of Poetry . . . the First Era of German Poetry. [But] The Period of Manhood, with its Doubts and stormful Impetuosities soon came; when the Church, as we shall see, no longer with its pillars and dome encircled the whole flock; and men were not like singing birds, but like falcons and vultures, and tore our Existence with wounds which are not yet healed. [65]

Then, as the last sentence in the manuscript, Carlyle writes:

We must now bid these peaceful School-greens, and blithe Maypole rings of Boyhood and Youth adieu; and turn to the jostling marketplace and battlefield, where Men work out their being; and seldom, and only by effort realize that old harmony and peaceable completeness of soul, which then came almost of their own accord. [65]

In the uncompleted *History of German Literature*, naturally Carlyle says little of any era after the Middle Ages. The two passages just quoted from the last page of the manuscript show his hint of coming change, as he turned from the Swabian Era. A passage earlier quoted contrasts briefly the transcendental moral philosophy of the Twelfth Century with the materialistic moral philosophy of the Eighteenth Century. [66] But concerning the Nineteenth Century, he is hopeful: he shows his faith in a future that will be better than his own time. That new and better time is already traceable in German literature. Indeed, on all hands, he says, it begins to be understood that German literature

---

[64] *Ibid.*, p. 109. Carlyle's footnote assigns the quotation to " Tieck's *Minnelieder aus dem Schwäbischen Zeitalter* (*Vorrede* X) ."

[65] Manuscript *History of German Literature* (Manuscript Vault of Yale University Library), p. 110.

[66] *Ibid.*, p. 92.

is not only a clear melodious Echo of the present Time, but also a Prophecy of a new and better Time, traces and incipient form of which already lie revealed there.[67]

But this work, written in 1830, contains little about Democracy. In every country, he thinks, where there is free press, the government must become democratic. That is, whatever may be the technical form of government, the government must ultimately be rendered " a Democracy, and perhaps the only genuine and possible Democracy, reducing the duty of the Sovereign to that of a mere Policeman. . . ." [68]

In two respects the unpublished Volume I of the *History of German Literature* is Carlyle's closest approximation, before mid-1830, to his mature concept of historical periodicity. That is, in the first place, the *History* indicates briefly the Phoenix method of transition between successive eras. And, in the second place, it describes at length the Middle Ages, with the great directive principles, or organizing institutions, of Christianity and Chivalry. But, important as those two elements are, they are not bound together by any clear notion of progressive periodic mutation in which each successive period consists of alternate epochs of growth and decay. However, the letter-descriptions of his plan for the *History* show that he had acquired a tentative concept of historical periodicity. And his characterizations, in the letters, of alternate poetic and didactic epochs do, in a limited way, offer some analogies to his later characterizations of alternate epochs of belief and unbelief. The stress upon *belief* in the last epoch that he describes in the letters should especially be noted. But the dates that he there assigns to the five epochs within some seven centuries conform only in small part to the

[67] *Ibid.,* p. 12.   [98] *Ibid.,* p. 5.

dates that he is later to assign to epochs in his mature concept. In short, close as Carlyle had arrived by mid-1830 to parts of his mature concept of historical periodicity, his approximations seem fragmentary. It is safe to say that the whole sweep and implications of the mature concept were not yet clear in his mind. Brilliant insights were there, interspersed with gaps, and confused with tangential ideas.

Some of the noteworthy ideas that are related to the concept of periodicity found in Carlyle's writings before mid-1830 may profitably be recalled in another rapid summary. Though Carlyle in early 1830 called his alternate epochs by the terms *poetic* and *didactic,* he associated the element of belief, or faith, with the last-named of the poetic epochs. Even earlier, in addition to associating faith with Goethe and perhaps with the age of Goethe, he had characterized the Seventeenth Century, Milton's era, as an era of faith and the Eighteenth Century, Voltaire's era, as an era of skepticism. Furthermore this implied clash between belief and unbelief—a contrast set deep in Carlyle's moral philosophy—had first been rationalized in his mind by the distinction between *Vernunft* and *Verstand.* And, finally, the contrast between the dynamic and the mechanic in " Signs of the Times " is intimately bound up with the contrast between belief and unbelief and is in many respects congruent with the psychological distinction between reason and understanding. Thus all those points were in some way connected with Carlyle's notion of historical periodicity. And awareness of the relationship will help us in tracing the derivation and development of Carlyle's mature concept.

II

At this point, mid-1830, some two months before Carlyle had read any communications from the Saint-Simonians, the question arises as to the sources of his early concept. Doubtless in his wide reading he had encountered numerous treatments of historical periodicity.

Probably the most adequate English source of the various elements that have just been presented from Carlyle's thought is Coleridge. As already shown, the distinction between reason and understanding occupied an important place in Carlyle's early thought. And with it were connected his early attitudes toward faith and doubt and his elaborate contrast between dynamics and mechanics. In Coleridge's thought, too, the distinction between reason and understanding is fundamental, furnishing the key to much of Coleridge's mature philosophical, theological, and political writing.[69] And it is worth noting that Coleridge too makes an interesting, though not elaborate, contrast between dynamic and mechanic.[70] Furthermore Coleridge, like Carlyle, states his notion of progress [71] in terms of historical periodicity.

[69] See *The Friend* in Coleridge's *Works* (Philadelphia, Crissy and Markley, 1849), pp. 410, 416 footnote, 420; *Biographia Literaria* in *Works* (Philadelphia, Crissy and Markley, 1849), pp. 253, 264-265, 297; *Aids to Reflection* (sixth edition, revised and corrected, New York, Stanford and Swords, 1847), pp. 121, 127, 161-177, 187, 208 footnote; " A Course of Lectures [1818]," Lectures VIII and IX (in *Coleridge's Essays and Lectures on Shakspeare and Some Other Old Poets and Dramatists* [Everyman's Library edition, London, Dent, 1907], pp. 251-252, 259-264); and E. L. Griggs' article " *The Friend*: 1809 and 1818 Editions," *Modern Philology*, XXXV (May, 1938), 369-373. Carlyle's familiarity with, and use of, Coleridge's thought does not need demonstration here: see my " Carlyle and the German Philosophy Problem during the Year 1826-1827," *PMLA*, L (1935), 813-814.

[70] *Biographia Literaria*, Chapter IX (*The Works of Samuel Taylor Coleridge* [Philadelphia, Crissy and Markley, 1849], p. 267).

[71] Nikolaus Schanck, " Die Sozial-Politischen Anschauungen Coleridges

The progress of the species neither is nor can be like that
of a Roman road in a right line. It may be more justly
compared to that of a river . . . frequently forced back
towards its fountains . . . yet with an accompanying impulse that will ensure its advancement hereafter . . . .
something is unremittingly gaining, either in secret preparation or in open and triumphant progress. . . . A whole
generation may appear even to sleep . . . [but] scattered and
solitary minds are always laboring somewhere in the service
of truth and virtue. . . .[72]

Applying this theory of alternation, Coleridge shifts to
a contrast between light and dark. Chaucer's era, an
era of light, was followed by the War of the Roses, an
era of darkness. And " The hundred years that followed
the usurpation of Henry the Fourth, were a hurling-
back of the mind of the country. . . . "[72] Elsewhere in
The Friend Coleridge goes further in his use of the
concept of alternating epochs within historical periods.
He is discussing what he calls the two main directions
of human activity, commerce and literature, which he
believes are inseparably coexistent.

As is the rank assigned to each [commerce and literature]
in the theory and practice of the governing classes, and
according to its prevalence in forming the foundation of
their public habits and opinions, so will the outward and
inward life of the people at large; such will the nation be.
In tracing the epochs, and alternations of their relative
sovereignty or subjection, consists the PHILOSOPHY of His-

und sein Einfluss auf Carlyle," *Bonner Studien zur Englischen Philologie,*
Hft. 16 (1924), p. 55, notices concerning Coleridge and Carlyle: " Beide
haben Verständnis für den Fortschritt."

[72] *The Friend* in *Works* (Philadelphia, 1849), p. 488. True, Coleridge
is not always consistent in this point of view. In *Aids* (New York,
Stanford and Swords, 1847), p. 201, he says: " Nature is a line in con-
tant and continuous evolution." In the same work, *Aids,* pp. 82-83, he
seems to approach Herder's idea of evolution of organic life from inorganic matter. Professor G. R. Potter has a very interesting article on
" Coleridge and the Idea of Evolution," *PMLA,* XL (1925), 379-397.

tory. In the power of distinguishing and appreciating their several results consists the historic SENSE.[73]

However, when he came to touch briefly upon the history of German literature in *Biographia Literaria,*[74] Coleridge did not stress any succession of alternate epochs. Unavoidably his comments remind us that Carlyle was to attempt organizing some of the same materials early in 1830. Coleridge mentions some of the same writers and groups of writers, stresses the Swabian era, believes Luther began a new era in the German language, comments that the language declined into pedantry within a century after Luther, compares Opitz to Dryden, and admires the splendid era that began with Gellert, Klopstock, Ramler, and Lessing. But there is no tangible evidence that Carlyle's division of the seven centuries, from the Minnesingers to Goethe, into five alternate poetic and didactic epochs owes anything to Coleridge's rapid sketch.

In short, we may conclude that up to mid-1830 Carlyle's uses of the concept of historical periodicity bear some resemblance to Coleridge's uses of it. The two British writers' notions of a succession of alternate epochs of advance and recession in human history are at least in a general way similar. Certain similarities between the two writers' treatments of German literary history, though they require brief notice, seem to contain little that is significant in the present investigation. However, Carlyle's sharp contrast between mechanic and dynamic is based upon the distinction between

---

[73] *The Friend* in *Works* (Philadelphia, 1849), p. 523. A few pages earlier in the same work, Coleridge's comment on the French Revolution is strikingly like Carlyle's interpretation of it in the essay on Voltaire: " . . . the French revolution was, we hope, the closing *monsoon* . . ." of the spirit that was at work, during the latter half of the last century. *The Friend, ibid.,* p. 515.

[74] *Biographia Literaria,* Chapter X, *ibid.,* pp. 278-279.

understanding and reason, a distinction probably derived largely from Coleridge. Carlyle's attitude toward
faith was rationalized by the same distinction. And
later, as we shall soon see, this stress on faith, or belief,
which appeared in Carlyle's characterization of the last
poetic epoch of German literature, became a point of
great importance. But, granting some broad resemblances and even some important details of resemblance
between Carlyle's thought up to mid-1830, and Coleridge's thought, we must not suppose that the whole
problem is solved. Though, by mid-1830, Carlyle had
groped a considerable way toward his final concept of
historical periodicity, he had still a good way to go.
Though several of the elements involved in the concept
have been shown and even some of their developments
and combinations traced, they have not yet merged
into a thoroughly worked-out concept. Before they did
so merge, two more very important influences were to
join with Coleridge's to shape the concept.

In addition to the influence represented by Coleridge,
direct German influence had long played an important
part in Carlyle's thought. Indeed, one of the most distinguished of Carlyle scholars attributes Carlyle's mature concept of historical periodicity to this German
influence. After examining the various possible German
sources of the concept, Professor Harrold arrives at the
following conclusions.

In Schiller, Fichte, Novalis, Friedrich Schlegel, and Schel-
ling, he [Carlyle] could have found abundant effort at chart-
ing the past course of man's history according to some
principle which marked off and interpreted a series of
epochs.[75]

[75] C. F. Harrold, *Carlyle and German Thought: 1819-1834* (New
Haven, Yale University Press, 1934, *Yale Studies in English,* LXXXII),
p. 171.

Those writers, especially Fichte and Novalis, he says, familiarized Carlyle with the process of thinking of history in terms of periodic rhythms. But

it was Goethe, rather than any of the philosophers, who contributed most to Carlyle's notion of the rhythm of history. . . . [76] The well-known passage in Goethe, which supplied Carlyle with both the doctrine and the terms, is one which . . . occurs . . . in one of the *Notes* to the *West-Oestlicher Divan.*[77]

The Goethe passage thus alluded to runs as follows.

Das eigentliche, einzige und tiefste Thema der Welt- und Menschengeschichte, dem alle übrigen untergeordnet sind, bleibt der Konflikt des Unglaubens und Glaubens. Alle Epochen, in welchen der Glaube herrscht, unter welcher Gestalt er auch wolle, sind glänzend, herzerhebend und fruchtbar für Mitwelt und Nachwelt. Alle Epochen dagegen, in welchen der Unglaube, in welcher Form es sei, einen kümmerlichen Sieg behauptet, und wenn sie auch einen Augenblick mit einem Scheinglanze prahlen sollten, verschwinden vor der Nachwelt, weil sich niemand gern mit Erkenntnis des Unfruchtbaren abquälen mag.

Die vier letzten Bücher Mosis haben, wenn uns das erste den Triumph des Glaubens darstellte, den Unglauben zum Thema. . . .[78]

The Goethe passage just quoted is extremely important in our investigation. Carlyle may have known it [79]

---

[76] *Ibid.,* p. 171.   [77] *Ibid.,* p. 174.

[78] I have quoted from Goethe's Note "Israel in der Wüste," in *Sämmtliche Werke* (ed. K. Goedeke, Stuttgart, n. d.), III, 205. Professor Harrold, using the Jubiläums-Ausgabe, paraphrased the last sentence of the quotation thus: " Goethe suggests that ' the last four books of Moses' show the triumph of ' unfaith,' apathy, weakness, after a period of supremely positive action." And he summarized the main thought in the passage thus: "World-history, in general, Goethe concludes, shows this unceasing oscillation between faith and negation." Harrold, *Carlyle and German Thought: 1819-1834,* p. 297, note 57.

[79] He may have known it in the now rare 1819 (Stuttgart) edition of *West-Östlicher Divan,* or in *Goethe's Werke* (Wien, 1820), XXI, 376-406.

as early as March 1826.[80] And thus it may have cooperated with the various elements we have already
noticed in his early concept of periodicity. The Goethe
passage does include some of the principle and some of
the terms of Carlyle's mature concept. Therefore the
various elements in the quotation should be noticed in
detail. The quoted passage states the concept of periodic alternations of epochs of belief and epochs of doubt
in all human history. It impressively characterizes the
two sorts of epochs,—characterizes them in the exact
terminology that Carlyle was to use many times. And
it specifically designates one epoch of belief and one
epoch of doubt—both from Hebrew history. But it
does not apply the concept specifically to any part of
European history. It does not point out or discuss,
even for Hebrew history, any of the institutions or
schemata involved in the epochs. And it does not discuss the method of transition between historical periods.
The problem of influence must turn on all these elements; upon these last three, which are lacking in the

[80] In the Introduction (written in March 1826) to his translation of
Meister's *Wanderjahre* (*William Meister's Apprenticeship and Travels,*
I, 23), Carlyle referred to the *Divan* as graceful and expressive. By July
19, 1826 (*German Romance* [London, Chapman and Hall, 1898], II, 124–
125) he mentioned *West Östlicher Divan* by name and alluded to the
idea underlying it. On August 20, 1827 (*Correspondence between Goethe
and Carlyle*, p. 31) he thanked Goethe for the first installment (volumes
I-V) of the new edition of Goethe's *Werke,* of which Volume V included
the *Divan* but not the *Noten.* By March 7, 1828 (see *Essays,* I, 146,
footnote), Carlyle was writing an essay that purported to review those
first five volumes. By the end of May 1828 (*Essays,* I, 198, footnote)
he had reviewed the second installment (volumes VI-X) of the *Werke,*
of which Volume VI included the *Noten.* He said (*Essays,* I, 198) that
this second installment contained nothing new to him. And again, about
July 13, 1832 (*Essays,* II, 431), he commented on the deep all-prevading
Faith that speaks forth in *Wanderjahre, West-Östlicher Divan,* and *Zahme
Xenien.* Though Carlyle thus knew the *Divan* by March, 1826, it is a
curious fact that he first specifically mentioned the " Israel in der
Wüste " passage in the summer of 1832.

Goethe passage, as well as upon the first three elements, which are very strikingly present.

Unquestionably every feature in that quotation from Goethe eventually became indelibly impressed upon Carlyle's mind. In order to establish that fact it seems proper to sacrifice temporarily the chronological sequence, which is strictly adhered to everywhere else in this study, and to present now some evidence of the long-continued influence of the Goethe passage on Carlyle's writings. At least a dozen passages in Carlyle's writings from 1831 on, show the imprint.[81] A few will suffice now. The earliest of them occurs in *Sartor,* which was finished by August 4, 1831.

As in long-drawn systole and long-drawn diastole, must the period of Faith alternate with the period of Denial; must the vernal growth, the summer luxuriance of all Opinions, Spiritual Representations and Creations, be followed by,

---

[81] There may be some advantages in seeing, all at one time, the locations and dates of these passages: (1) *Sartor Resartus* (ed. C. F. Harrold, New York, Doubleday, Doran and Company, 1937), p. 112 (by August 4, 1831); (2) J. A. Froude, *Thomas Carlyle: A History of the First Forty Years of His Life: 1795-1835* (New York, Scribner's, 1882), II, 230-231 (between July 22 and August 8, 1832); (3) *ibid.,* II, 249 (August 11, 1832); (4) "Diderot," *Essays,* III, 248 (by October 15, 1832); (5) *The French Revolution. A History* (Centenary Edition, London, Chapman and Hall, 1898), I, 10-11 (1835); (6) *ibid.,* III, 119 (by January 12, 1837); (7) *Lectures on the History of Literature* (ed. R. P. Karkaria, London, Curwen, Kane and Co., 1892), p. 54; (8) *On Heroes, Hero-Worship and the Heroic in History* (London, Chapman and Hall, 1898), p. 77 (delivered May, 1840; published April, 1841); (9) *ibid.,* p. 126; (10) *ibid.,* p. 172; (11) *ibid.,* p. 204; (12) *Oliver Cromwell's Letters and Speeches, with Elucidations* (London, Chapman and Hall, 1897), I, 83-84 (finished August, 1845). Each of these passages from Carlyle shows, both in thought and in diction, distinct influence of the Goethe passage. Professor Harrold (*Carlyle and German Thought: 1819-1834,* pp. 175, 176, 297), who was not attempting to multiply instances, pointed out the passages here numbered, 1, 4, and 11. The other passages have been noted here in the effort to show how pervasive the influence was.

and again follow, the autumnal decay, the winter dis-solution.[82]

And Carlyle's writings during the next year, 1832, con-tain two passages that are avowed translations from the Goethe Note. The first of them, written in Carlyle's notebook between July 22nd and August 8th, includes all except the last sentence of the Goethe passage just quoted.

' The special, sole, and deepest theme of the world's and man's history, whereto all other themes are subordinated, remains the conflict of unbelief and belief. All epochs wherein belief prevails, under what form it will, are splendid, heart-elevating, fruitful for contemporaries and posterity. All epochs, on the contrary, where unbelief, in what form soever, maintains its sorry victory, should they even for a moment glitter with a sham splendour, vanish from the eyes of posterity, because no one chooses to burden himself with a study of the unfruitful.'—' Goethe's Works,' vi, 159, on Moses and his Exodus.[83]

The second translation, which occurs in the essay " Diderot," [84] finished by October 15, 1832, is an almost identical copy of the first, or notebook, version.[85] This second, or " Diderot," passage Carlyle attributes merely

---

[82] *Sartor Resartus*, p. 112, where Professor Harrold again calls atten-tion to the influence of Goethe, and says that this theory of alternate ages of faith and doubt became a part of Carlyle's phoenix doctrine. But we must remember that the phoenix doctrine is not expressed in the Goethe passage. Attention has already been called to Carlyle's notice of the phoenix figure in connection with Werner's religious faith, and to his more important use of the figure to suggest the method of transition between eras in the unpublished *History of German Literature*.

[83] Froude, *Thomas Carlyle . . . 1795-1835*, II, 230-231. The quotation marks occur in the text.

[84] *Essays*, III, 248.

[85] In the two 1832 versions, the thought is the same. There are slight differences in punctuation and in capitalization. A few of the words are changed: *will* in notebook, *may* in essay; *where, wherein; in, under; a study, study*.

to " the Thinker of our time." A final proof of the extent to which the excerpt had fused with other elements in Carlyle's thought before the decade was over is found in the *Lectures* of 1838. In these *Lectures*, Carlyle was speaking, not reading. Although Carlyle assigned the passage to Goethe and although the editor of the *Lectures* therefore inclosed the passage in quotation marks, Carlyle's rendering of 1838 is obviously a free or adapted one.

' . . . Belief and Unbelief are two opposite principles in human nature. The theme of all human history, as far as we are able to perceive it, is the contest between these two principles.' ' All periods,' he [Goethe] goes on to say, ' in which Belief predominates, in which it is the main element, the inspiring principle of action, are distinguished by great, soul stirring, fertile events, and worthy of perpetual remembrance. And, on the other hand, when unbelief gets the upper hand, that age is unfertile, unproductive, and intrinsically mean, in which there is no pabulum for the Spirit of man, and no one can get nourishment for himself.' This passage is one of the most pregnant utterances ever delivered, and we shall do well to keep it in mind in these disquisitions on this [medieval] period. For in the Middle Ages we see the great phenomenon of Belief gaining the victory over Unbelief. And this same remark is altogether true of all things whatever in this world; it throws much light on the history of the whole world, and that in two ways: for Belief serves both as a fact itself, and the cause of other facts. It appears only in a healthy mind and is at once an indication of it and the cause of it.[86]

There is no need to proceed now through the other available Carlyle passages to prove that, by the late 1830's, the passage from Goethe had been thoroughly assimilated into Carlyle's own thought.

---

[86] *Lectures on the History of Literature,* p. 54. Quotation marks occur in the text. See also p. 192 for Carlyle's very high opinion of Goethe's *West-Östlicher Divan.*

Certainly assimilated by 1838, when Carlyle was de-
livering his *Lectures on the History of Literature*,
Goethe's influence just noticed may have been active
by 1830, when Carlyle was trying to write his *History of
German Literature*. By mid-1830, though Carlyle had
not gone as far as had Goethe in stating the theory that
history is an alternation of epochs of belief and doubt,
he had gone beyond Goethe in applying a concept of
periodicity to European history. But even with the aid
of English Coleridge and German Goethe, Carlyle had
nowhere, by mid-1830, set forth the full concept of
historical periodicity that was to appear in his later
works.

CHAPTER II

The Saint-Simonian Concept of Historical Periodicity

The contributors of the elements that were still lacking to make up Carlyle's mature concept of periodicity were the French Saint-Simonians. And they, who were likewise the contributors of the elaborate systematization of the concept in such a way as to include or to harmonize the various elements already noted, were soon to swim into Carlyle's ken.

The elaborate Saint-Simonian concept of historical periodicity occurs with much stress and with frequent repetition in many of the Saint-Simonian writings extending over a period of years. In order to avoid confusion in presenting this complicated concept, it seems best to draw the concept into its smallest compass and to relegate to footnotes the mosaic of exact quotations. As we proceed into this digest of the Saint-Simonian concept, it will suffice to say that all of the materials from which it is drawn came before Carlyle and were diligently studied by him within a short period beginning August, 1830, and extending for perhaps as long as a year and a half. The facts of how the materials came before him and the facts concerning his reactions to them will be considered in full detail later in this study. Just now our purpose is to show as simply as possible the concept of periodicity that Carlyle during 1830-1831 found in the Saint-Simonian writings.

The concept of periodicity that Carlyle found in the Saint-Simonian literature in 1830-1831 can be analyzed into five main features: (1) Statement of the law of progressive periodic mutation, (2) Characterization of the two kinds of epochs in each period, (3) Definition of the method of transition between periods, (4) Designation of the two complete periods in past European history, and (5) Interpretation of the present and the future in the light of periodicity. We shall proceed with the exposition of each of those five features of the Saint-Simonian concept.

(1) Statement of the Law of Progressive Periodic Mutation.

To the philosopher of history, the past, the present, and the future are organic parts of a whole.[1] Therefore, principles may be observed and laws induced concerning the progress of civilization.[1] Humanity is indefinitely perfectible, and it unceasingly progresses.[2]

[1] For the philosopher, "l'histoire toute entière est dans les faits généraux qui, indiquant la marche de la civilisation antérieure, peuvent servir à expliquer la civilisation actuelle, et à pressentir celle qui lui succédera." (*Le Producteur, Journal de l'industrie, des sciences et des beaux-arts*, II, 538. Published in Paris, 1825-1826, 5 volumes. Hereafter referred to as *Le Producteur*. The passage just quoted was written by P. M. L. [i. e., P. M. Laurent].)

". . . il s'agissait de chercher dans l'observation des faits du passé, les lois du progrès ou du développement de l'espèce humaine." (*Le Producteur*, IV, 402. The article was written by Bazard.)

[2] "L'humanité est indéfiniment perfectible." (*L'Organisateur, Journal des progrès de la science générale*, 1st year, no. 50 [July 24, 1830], p. 1. This weekly periodical, averaging, during its last year, some eight pages to the issue, was published at Paris from August 15, 1829, to August 15, 1831. On April 18, 1830, it adopted the subtitle *Journal de la doctrine de Saint-Simon*. This periodical will hereafter be referred to as *L'Organisateur*. This *L'Organisateur* of 1829-1831 should not be confused with *L'Organisateur* of 1819. There is no definite proof that Carlyle knew the 1819 publication. The points of similarity between Carlyle's work and the 1819 publication, which I have examined, could have been derived from the 1829-1831 publication, which Carlyle is known to have read.)

The law of perfectibility glimpsed by Condorcet and Kant has been "positivement établie par St.-Simon." (*Le Producteur*, III, 10. The article was written by Enfantin.)

". . . Kant en Allemagne, et surtout Condorcet en France, par la

But while progressing, it follows a law of periodicity. That is, humanity progresses, not by one continuous forward movement, but by an alternating movement in

manière dont ils ont présenté l'idée de perfectibilité, avaient conçu la possibilité d'établir une philosophie de l'histoire, devant servir de base à la théorie de l'organisation sociale." (*Le Producteur,* III, 87-88. The article was written by O. R. [Olinde Rodrigues].) In a later article (*Le Producteur,* III, 288-289), O. R. says that, in comparing the development of the human spirit in general with the development of the faculties of an individual, Condorcet did not prove *à posteriori* his *aperçu,* or amplify it, or draw any remarkable consequences from it. On the other hand (says O. R., pp. 289-290), observation formed the basis of Saint-Simon's belief that the general intelligence and the individual intelligence develop according to the same law. And that law " offre l'avantage de pouvoir connaître le sort futur de l'humanité."

"Nous avons dit: 'L'humanité est un être collectif, se développant dans la succession des générations, comme l'individu se développe dans la succession des âges. Son développement est progressif." (*Exposition de la doctrine Saint-Simonienne. Deuxième année.* Originally published Paris, 1830. Re-published, 1877, in Vol. XLII of *Oeuvres de Saint-Simon et d'Enfantin.* Publiées par les membres du conseil institué par Enfantin pour l'exécution de ses dernières volontés. Paris, 1865-1878. 47 volumes. Hereafter referred to as *Exposition,* 2nd year (*Oeuvres,* XLII). The quotation just given is from the 1st seance, p. 153. Ten of the thirteen lectures that constitute this *Exposition,* 2nd year, were published in the weekly *L'Organisateur* between December 20, 1829, and July 13, 1830. The three omitted were lectures 6, 7, and 9. Though I find no definite proof that Carlyle knew the *Exposition,* 2nd year, in book form, he surely knew *L'Organisateur.* The two versions of the ten lectures I have not collated carefully; but, so far as I know, for the purposes of this study, they are essentially the same. *L'Organisateur* of course contains much material besides the lectures).

"Grâce aux travaux de quelques hommes supérieurs du XVIIIᵉ siècle, la croyance à la perfectibilité *indéfinie* de l'espèce humaine est aujourd'hui généralement répandue. . . . [Here and hereafter the italics are in the text. The passage continues in a new paragraph, thus:]

"L'idée de *perfectibilité,* entrevue par Vico, Lessing, Turgot, Kant, Herder, Condorcet, est restée stérile dans leurs mains, parce qu'aucun de ces philosophes n'a su *caractériser* le progrès; aucun d'eux n'a indiqué *en quoi* il consistait, *comment* il s'était opéré, par *quelles institutions* il s'était produit et devait se continuer; aucun d'eux, en présence des faits nombreux de l'histoire, n'a su les classer en faits *progressifs* et faits *rétrogrades,* les coordonner en séries *homogènes* dont tous les termes fussent enchaînés suivant une loi de *croissance* ou de *décroissance.* . . ." (*Doctrine de Saint-Simon. Exposition première année,* 1829. [First edition,

two phases.[3] Those two opposite phases of humanity's progress are called the organic epochs of history, on one hand, and the critical epochs of history, on the other.[3] Thus humanity has described one period in its history when it has passed through one organic epoch and one critical epoch.

(2) Characterization of the Two Kinds of Epochs in Each Period.

(a) The organic epochs are so-named because of the completeness of their organization around basic sche-

Paris, 1830.] Nouvelle édition, publiée avec introduction et notes par C. Bouglé et Elie Halévy, Paris, Marcel Rivière, 1924. Hereafter referred to as *Exposition*, 1st year. My references are to the 1924 edition. The passage just quoted is from the 2nd seance, p. 166, footnote).

Herder and Condorcet and others believed in perfectibility, but Saint-Simon alone worked out a division of history into organic and critical epochs. (*L'Organisateur*, 2nd year, no. 51 [August 6, 1831], p. 394.)

Note that the Saint-Simonians stressed their contact with the various intellectual currents in Europe. In Carlyle's eyes, they perhaps gained some prestige through their familiarity with Kant, whom they treated as a forerunner of their concept of historical periodicity (*Le Producteur*, III, 87-88). Their modern editors (Bouglé and Halévy, *Exposition*, 1st year, pp. 500-501, note) point out in some detail the avenues of connection between the Saint-Simonians and Kant and Hegel. See also *Oeuvres*, II, 170, and *Le Producteur*, IV, 403.

[3] History shows us that humanity " marche sans cesse à son perfectionnement, à son perfectionnement *trinitaire*, à la fois *moral*, *scientifique* et *industriel*." But it also shows us, at the same time, that this "perfectionnement" does not operate in a continuous manner. Humanity passes alternately through organic and critical (religious and irreligious) epochs. (*L'Organisateur*, 1st year, no. 20 [December 27, 1829] p. 3.)

" Cette loi [i. e. la loi du développement de l'humanité] constatée par l'étude de l'histoire, nous montre la société passant alternativement par deux états distincts: l'un, que nous appelons *état organique* ou *normal*, sous l'empire duquel tous les faits de l'activité humaine sont classés, prévus et soumis à une théorie générale, et où le but social est nettement défini; l'autre, que nous désignons sous le nom d'*état critique*, dans lequel les individus, luttant contre des dogmes usés, abjurent de plus en plus l'esprit d'association, en croyant ne l'attaquer d'abord que dans ses formes surannées, et finissent par se perdre dans le néant moral de l'égoïsme." (*L'Organisateur*, 1st year, no. 1 [August 15, 1829], p. 3.)

mata. In an organic epoch, human activities are inspired by one directive principle.[4] They conform to one frame (*cadre*), or system, or general theory.[4] And they cooperate in one common end.[4] In these organic epochs, men believe that the phenomena of life are ruled by a beneficient will [4] And all organic epochs are essentially religious.[5]

[4] See the last quotation in *Note 3,* immediately above. Also, "Les époques organiques sont celles où la société considérée toujours dans les populations les plus avancés, est régie par un principe commun." (*L'Organisateur,* 1st year, no. 17 [December 6, 1829], p. 2.)

Organic (or religious) epochs are those in which the facts of human activity are "ordonnés" by a general theory, and society tends toward one end. (*Ibid.,* 2nd year, no. 51 [August 6, 1831], p. 394.)

"Les spécialités diverses dont elles [the sciences] se composent ne se présentent, aux époques organiques, que comme une série de sous-divisions de la conception générale du *dogme* fondamental. Il y a réellement alors *encyclopédie* des sciences, en conservant à ce mot, encyclopédie, sa véritable signification, c'est-à-dire, enchaînement des connaissances humaines." (*Exposition,* 1st year, 3rd séance, p. 197.)

"Aux époques organiques, le but de l'activité *sociale* est nettement défini; tous les efforts, avons-nous dit, sont consacrés à l'accomplissement de ce but, vers lequel les hommes sont continuellement dirigés, dans le cours entier de leur vie, par l'éducation et la législation. Les relations générales étant fixées, les relations individuelles, modelées sur elles, le sont également; l'objet que la société se propose d'atteindre est révélé à tous les coeurs, à toutes les intelligences . . . .

"L'homme alors voit l'ensemble des phénomènes régi par une providence, par une volonté bienfaisante . . . . On peut dire, en ce sens, que le caractère des époques organiques est essentiellement *religieux.*" (*Ibid.,* p. 196.)

[5] . . . toutes les époques *organiques* ont été *religieuses,* dans le sens ordinairement attaché à ce mot, c'est-à-dire reliées en Dieu, . . . toutes les époques *critiques* ont été *irreligieuses*: si bien qu'ordre et religion, désordre et irreligion sont synonymes." (*L'Organisateur,* 2nd year, no. 28 [February 26, 1831], p. 221.)

". . . époques *Organiques* ou religieuses . . . ." (*Aux Artistes. Du passé et de l'avenir des beaux-arts* [Paris, A. Mesnier, 1830], p. 6. This unsigned pamphlet is by E. Barrault.)

"Les époques organiques présentent en outre un caractère général qui domine tous ces caractères particuliers; elles sont RELIGIEUSES. La religion est alors la synthèse de toute l'activité humaine, individuelle et sociale." (*Exposition,* 2nd year, 1st séance [*Oeuvres,* XLII, 156].)

". . . l'on peut dire que dans toute époque organique la science a été

(b) The critical epochs, on the other hand, are named for their questioning or critical attitude toward the fundamental schemata. In a critical epoch, the old regulative principle, frame, or aim has ceased to be harmonious with the facts of science and with the needs of society.[6] New facts have emerged, and society has felt new needs that cannot be included in the narrow, inflexible frame (*cadre*) of the old creeds and institutions.[7] Humanity cannot be bound in absolute and unchangeable forms. So the old creeds and institutions become the targets of attack.[6] Eventually the new facts, by repeated collision, shake the old order from its foundations and overturn it.[7] For a while, until the old religious and social institutions are overturned, society unites in the labor of destruction.[8] At such times,

théologique, puisque c'était dans le temple et par les prêtres qu'elle était cultivée." (*Exposition*, 1st year, 14th séance, p. 436.)

" Tous les anciens dogmes religieux sont, au fond, une transformation sentimentale des premiers aperçus scientifiques de l'humanité . . . . " (*Le Producteur*, III, 296. The article is by O. R. [Olinde Rodrigues].)

" . . . tout état organique des sociétés humaines était la conséquence, la représentation d'une CONCEPTION RELIGIEUSE. . . . on pourrait dire que l'HOMME EST UN ÊTRE RELIGIEUX QUI SE DÉVELOPPE." (*Exposition*, 2nd year, 7th séance [*Oeuvres*, XLII, 283]. There is no positive proof that Carlyle knew this 7th séance of the 2nd year: see *ante*, note 2.)

[6] " Les époques critiques sont celles où le principe régulateur a cessé d'être en harmonie avec les besoins de la société, et devient le but de toutes les attaques des hommes supérieurs, de toutes les antipathies des masses." (*L'Organisateur*, 1st year, no. 17 [December 6, 1829], p. 2.)

[7] " Lorsqu'arrive le temps des époques *critiques* ou de destruction, c'est que des faits *nouveaux* se sont produits; c'est que la société éprouve des besoins nouveaux, que ne comporte pas et que ne peut comprendre le cadre trop étroit, et devenu inflexible, de la croyance établie et de l'institution politique qui la réalise. Cependant ces faits nouveaux, ces exigences d'avenir, cherchent à se faire jour, à prendre place; d'abord ils viennent se briser contre l'ordre ancien; mais, par leur choc répété, ils finissent par l'ébranler et par le renverser lui-même." (*Exposition*, 1st year, 13th séance, p. 410.)

[8] " . . . les époques critiques se divisent en deux périodes distinctes: l'une formant le début de ces époques, pendant laquelle la société, ralliée par une foi vive aux doctrines de destruction, agit de concert pour

even men born to love their fellowmen have to conse-
crate their lives to hate and destruction. Eventually
cooperation, even for destruction, is replaced by the
moral negation, egoism.[9] The old theoretical synthesis
that unified and interpreted man's experience, has disappeared.[10] All critical epochs are essentially irreligious.[11]

(3) Definition of the Method of Transition between
Epochs or Periods.

renverser l'ancienne institution religieuse et sociale; l'autre, comprenant
l'intervalle qui sépare la destruction de la réédification, pendant laquelle
les hommes, dégoûtés du passé et incertains de l'avenir, ne sont plus unis
par aucune foi, par aucune entreprise communes: ce que nous avons dit
de l'absence de moralité aux époques critiques, ne doit s'entendre que de
la seconde des deux périodes qu'elles comprennent, mais non point de la
première, non point des hommes qui y figurent et qui, par une sorte
d'inconséquence, prêchent la haine par amour, appellent la destruction en
croyant édifier, provoquent le désorde parce qu'ils désirent l'ordre,
établissent l'esclavage sur l'autel qu'ils élèvent à la liberté.   Ceux-là,
Messieurs, sachons les admirer, plaignons-les seulement d'avoir été soumis
à la mission terrible qu'ils ont remplie avec dévoûment, avec amour pour
l'humanité; plaignons-les, car ils étaient nés pour aimer et toute leur
vie a été consacrée à la haine." (*Ibid.*, 1st year, 13th séance, pp. 412-
413.)

[9] In the era " que nous désignons sous le nom d'*état critique* . . . les
individus, luttant contre des dogmes usés, abjurent de plus en plus l'esprit
d'association, en croyant ne l'attaquer d'abord que dans ses formes surannées, et finissent par se perdre dans le néant moral de l'égoisme."
(*L'Organisateur*, 1st year, no. 1 [August 15, 1829], p. 3.)

[10] In the " *état critique* . . . toute communion de pensée, toute action
d'ensemble, toute coordination a cessé, et . . . la société ne présente plus
qu'une agglomération d'individus isolés et luttant les uns contre les
autres." (*Exposition*, 1st year, 1st séance, p. 127.)

[11] See *ante, Note 3*.
Also note the expression " époques *Critiques* ou irréligieuses . . . ."
(*Aux Artistes*, p. 6.)
" . . . l'irréligion . . . forme le caractère général de notre époque,
comme de toutes les époques *critiques* . . . ." (*Exposition*, 2nd year, 1st
séance [*Oeuvres*, XLII, 171].)
" . . . les époques critiques sont IRRELIGIEUSES." (*Ibid.*, 2nd year, 1st
séance [*Oeuvres*, XLII, 156].)
In critical (irreligious) epochs the general theory is no longer admitted;
it becomes the object of all attacks. (*L'Organisateur*, 2nd year, no. 51
[August 6, 1831], p. 394.)

The transition between successive periods is gradual, each era containing in itself the germ of its successors— each old order producing the elements that destroy it.[12] That destruction of the old forms is necessary to the realization of new and better forms.[13] And the destruction of the old and the preparation of the new proceed at the same time.[14] The critical epoch lasts until a new principle of order is revealed to the world.[15] The regeneration that occurs at the end of a critical epoch is called *palingenesia*.[16] With *palingenesia*, begins a new organic epoch of a new historical period.

[12] " Chaque nouvelle ère est contenue en germe dans la précédente, elle en dérive comme une fille de sa mère, mais elle n'en est pas la prolongation." (*Ibid.*, 1st year, no. 20 [December 27, 1829], p. 3.)

[13] It was necessary that the old order fall into decrepitude " pendant que le nouveau se préparait." (*Ibid.*)

After commenting on organic and critical epochs and saying that the latter are full of disorder and the breaking-up of old social relations, the seance continues: " Ajoutons toutefois que celles-ci [critical epochs] furent toujours utiles, nécessaires, indispensables, puisqu'en détruisant des formes vieillies, qui nuisaient, après y avoir longtemps contribué, au développement de l'humanité, elles facilitèrent la conception et la réalisation de formes meilleures." (*Exposition*, 1st year, 2nd séance, p. 161.)

[14] While the Voltairean critique applied the last strokes to a past that was falling in ruins, "l'intelligence plus calme préparait les voies de l'avenir, en recherchant le principe qui devait présider à la reconstruction de l'édifice social. . . . C'était, comme nous l'avons vu, dans la passé qu'il fallait découvrir ce principe, car il avait nécessairement agi lui-même pour miner sourdement celui q'il devait remplacer . . . ." (*Le Producteur*, III, 85. The article is by Enfantin.)

[15] " . . . époques *critiques*, dans lesquelles l'ordre ancien est *critiqué*, attaqué, détruit, et qui s'étendent jusqu'au moment où un nouveau principe d'ordre est révélé au monde." (*Exposition*, 1st year, 3rd séance, p. 194.)

" A chaque révolution philosophique, religieuse et morale, il s'opère une nouvelle coordination des idées qui font la base du gouvernement populaire, du gouvernement universel. Il faut refaire le catéchisme, le livre élémentaire par excellence, pour le mettre en harmonie avec les progrès de l'esprit humain . . . ." (*Le Producteur*, III, 302. The article is by O. R. [Olinde Rodrigues].)

[16] " . . . la fin d'une de ces crises *palingénésiques* où s'opère le passage

(4) Designation of the Two Periods in Past European History.

The concept just presented—of alternate organic and critical epochs, one passing gradually into the other— the Saint-Simonians trace through many centuries of actual European history.[17] They go back to early

d'une époque critique épuissée, à une époque organique nouvelle . . . . " (*Exposition*, 1st year, 14th séance, p. 433.)

" L'Ecriture, dans le tableau du Déluge, nous a donné un magnifique *symbole* de la manière dont s'opèrent les régénérations, les *palingénésies* de la société." (*L'Organisateur*, 1st year, no. 20 [December 27, 1829], p. 3.)

The word *palingénésie* is used elsewhere by the Saint-Simonians in their discussion of the regeneration of society that takes place at the end of a critical epoch: e. g., *L'Organisateur*, 1st year, no. 21 [January 3, 1830], p. 5; and the translator's notice in *L'Education du genre humain*, de Lessing, traduit, pour la première fois, de l'Allemand, par Eugène Rodrigues (original edition was published at Paris, 1829. The edition I used was published at Paris, 1832; it is bound with Saint-Simon's *Nouveau Christianisme*), p. 302. See also Bouglé and Halévy's footnote to *Exposition*, 1st year, p. 279. The Saint-Simonians derived the word, it seems, from Ballanche (see Bouglé and Halévy's note just cited; see also Enfantin's letter to Ballanche, quoted in *Oeuvres*, II, 38; see also *Exposition*, 1st year, 14th séance, p. 433.)

[17] Jetons les yeux sur la série de civilisation à laquelle nous nous rattachons directement, et qui nous est la mieux connue. Elevés au milieu des lettres greques et romaines, fils de chrétiens, témoins du déclin du catholicisme, et de la tiédeur même de la réforme, deux périodes critiques nettement prononcées nous apparaissent dans la durée de vingt-trois siècles: 1° celle qui sépare le polythéisme du christianisme, c'est-à-dire qui s'étendit depuis l'apparition des premiers philosophes de la Grèce jusqu'à la prédication de l'Evangile; 2° celle qui sépare la doctrine catholique de celle de l'avenir, et qui comprend les trois siècles écoulés depuis LUTHER jusqu'à nos jours. Les époques organiques correspondantes sont: 1° celle où le polythéisme grec et romain fut dans la plus grande vigueur, et qui se termine aux siècles de PÉRICLÈS et d'AUGUSTE; 2° celle où le catholicisme et la féodalité furent constitués avec le plus de force et d'éclat, et qui vint finir, sous le rapport religieux, à LÉON X, sous le point de vue politique, à LOUIS XIV." (*Exposition*, 1st year, 3rd séance, pp. 194-195.)

The Saint-Simonians have not been able to study the development of one of the human faculties, says Barrault, without taking account of the influence of each of the great religious conceptions that have presided " à ses progrès," . . . " soit que cette conception, d'abord vigoureuse et puis-

Greece; and they come down to their own time. The stretch of time between—at least 2,300 years—they conceive as two complete historical periods. The first period is the Greek and Roman polytheistic period. It has its life cycle of growth and decay. That is, an organic epoch of polytheism is followed by a critical epoch, in which polytheism is broken down. The second period is the Catholic and feudal period. Its early organic epoch is likewise followed by critical breakdown. After it, will come a new organic epoch of a new, or third, historical period. Although the Saint-Simonians devote an increasing amount of attention to the centuries as they come nearer to their own time, they do go

sante, enfantât une *organisation*, soit qu' ébranlée et affaiblie, elle subit enfin une *crise* suivie de sa dissolution. De là, la division de l'histoire en époques *Organiques* ou religieuses, et en époques *Critiques* ou irréligieuses, division indispensable pour prévenir la confusion, et permettre de rapporter chaque effet à sa cause légitime. La série historique que ce travail embrasse présente deux époques organiques: la première constituée sous l'empire du polythéisme grec, la second sous celui du christianisme; et à la suite de ces époques organiques, deux époques critiques, dont l'une s'étend depuis l'ère philosophique des Grecs jusqu'à l'avènement du christianisme, et l'autre depuis la fin du quinzième siècle jusqu'à nous jours." (*Aux Artistes*, pp. 5-6.)

" . . . l'histoire, depuis l'antiquité grecque jusqu'à nos jours, présente tour à tour deux époques distinctes, l'une *Organique*, l'autre *Critique*. Des caractères de la première sont marqués le polythéisme et le moyen âge; de ceux de la seconde l'interrègne qui suivit chacun de ces états sociaux. L'histoire des arts, envisagée, dans la même série de faits, devra nous offrir successivement deux époques correspondantes." (*Ibid.*, pp. 12-13.)

Some other striking passages from the Saint-Simonians, insisting that the twenty-three centuries show two complete periods made up of alternating organic and critical epochs, and identifying and characterizing the epochs, will be found in later notes.

Comte, who wrote for *Le Producteur*, insisted that the human spirit describes successively three stages of theory: (1) theological (which is provisional), (2) metaphysical (which is also transitory), and (3) positive (which is definitive). And he held that the fundamental law of the human spirit thus constituted in three steps should be the point of departure of all philosophic research on man and on society. (*Le Producteur*, I, 348.)

into considerable detail about each epoch of each period,
particularizing it and dating it.

The first organic epoch of pagan polytheism extended
up to the Periclean Age of Greece and to the Augustan
Age of Rome.[18] (Note the dichotomy with respect to
Greek and Roman culture.)

After that first organic epoch, a critical epoch fol-
lowed. This first critical epoch dated from Socrates in
Greece and from the first century of the Empire in
Rome.[19] During this first critical epoch, the Olympian
Gods were dethroned, and the Roman Empire became
demoralized.[20]

Out of the dissolution of the pagan polytheistic world,
arose Christianity.[21] And Christianity became the regulative principle of the second organic epoch. This second
organic epoch was characterized by the Catholic system
in religion and by the feudal system in polity.[22] (Note
still another dichotomy,—this time, with respect to reli-

[18] See *ante,* note 17.
 Also, " Le polythéisme forme le premier état normal de cette période
historique." (*L'Organisateur,* 1st year, no. 1 [August 15, 1829], p. 3.)
 [19] The first critical epoch " s'étend depuis l'ère philosophique des Grecs
jusqu'à l'avènement du christianisme . . . ." (*Aux Artistes,* p. 6.)
 [20] The first critical epoch known dates back to the establishment of
the philosophic institutes in Greece. In that era the Olympian gods were
attacked and dethroned, and place was made for the " Dieu miséricordieux
des chrétiens." (*L'Organisateur,* 1st year, no. 1 [August 15, 1829],
p. 3.)
 The end of the first century of the Roman Empire was a time of great
demoralization: " Toute RELIGION, toute MORALE, tout ORDRE SOCIAL,
avaient disparu . . . ." (*Exposition,* 2nd year, 2nd séance [*Oeuvres,*
XLII, 184-185].)
 [21] The Olympian Gods were attacked and dethroned, and place was
made for the " Dieu miséricordieux des chrétiens." " La seconde époque
organique commence à la fondation de l'Eglise . . . ." (*L'Organisateur,*
1st year, no. 1 [August 15, 1829], p. 3).
 " Au milieu de l'oeuvre elle-même de la dissolution romaine, cette
religion régénératrice [i. e., Christianity] se produisit." (*Exposition,*
2nd year, 2nd séance [*Oeuvres,* XLII, 185-186].)
 [22] See *ante,* note 17.

gion and polity.) This second organic epoch extended from the establishment of the Church to the age of Leo X in religion and to the reign of Louis XIV in politics.[22]

After that second organic epoch, of Catholicism and feudalism, came the second critical epoch. This second critical epoch extended from Luther,[23] through Voltaire,[24] and to the present (1830).[25] Not until the

[23] Luther began the most recent critical epoch. (*L'Organisateur*, 1st year, no. 17 [December 6, 1829], p. 2.)

"La destruction du système féodal et théologique que Luther avait commencée trois siècles auparavant [i. e., before Saint-Simon], venait d'être consommée par la révolution française." (*L'Organisateur*, 1st year, no. 22 [January 20, 1830], p. 1.)

Saint-Simon himself accorded Luther only qualified admiration. That is, he said that the first, or critical phase of Luther's work—his destruction of Catholicism—was a capital service to civilization; but that the second, the organic or constructive, part left much to Luther's successors. Luther's protestantism, Saint-Simon felt, was merely another heresy; and that second phase of his work caused Christianity to retrograde. (C. H. deR. Saint-Simon, *Nouveau Christianisme* [original edition, Paris, 1825. References in this study are to the Paris edition of 1832], pp. 46-48, 65-66.)

[24] ". . . la féodalité n'a pas péri davantage sous la faux *du temps*, c'est la doctrine critique, commencée à la réforme religieuse et terminée d'une manière si brillante par Voltaire, qui a rebaissé toutes les supériorités nées de la conquête." (*Le Producteur*, III, 8. The article is by Enfantin.)

"L'imagination armée de la critique Voltairienne portait les derniers coups au passé tombant en ruines . . . ." (*Ibid.*, III, 85. The article is by Enfantin.)

"Au dix-huitième siècle, il n'en existait plus que les ruines [of the feudal edifice]; il était impossible de les relever. . . ." (*L'Industrie. Ou Discussions politiques, morales et philosophiques.* Par H. Saint-Simon [and others. Paris, 1817-1818. 4 volumes bound in 3. References are usually to a microphotographic reproduction of the files in Bibliothèque Nationale, Paris; however, a few passages are taken from the more accessible reprints in *Oeuvres de Saint-Simon et d'Enfantin*, Vol. XIX], II, 286.)

The philosophers struck at the old system; "le système des idées générales s'écroula tout entier et la société fut dissoute." (*L'Industrie*, II, 281.)

[25] ". . . les réformateurs du quinzième siècle ont ouvert la nouvelle

violent social crisis of the French Revolution was the eternal decree executed against the social order that was based upon the medieval theological system and feudalism.[26] Eighteenth Century liberalism, individualism, and democracy were valuable only to help demolish the old institutions and the creeds.[27] For the

ère critique que nous subissons encore, aussi misérable dans son déclin qu'elle fut généreuse dans son principe." (*L'Organisateur*, 1st year, no. 1 [August 15, 1829], p. 3.)

The second critical epoch " s'étend . . . depuis la fin du quinzième siècle jusqu'à nos jours." (*Aux Artistes*, p. 6.)

[26] See *ante*, note 24.

Also, " La génération de 1789 avait rempli sa mission: destinée à exécuter les décrets éternels contre l'ordre féodal, elle s'était montrée magnanime puis implacable, selon la nécessité des temps . . . ." (*Le Globe*, 7th year, no. 3 [January 3, 1831], p. 1281. *Le Globe*, a daily begun at Paris in 1824, had as its subtitle *Journal philosophique et littéraire*. In November 1830 it became a Saint-Simonian organ. [See A. J. Booth, *Saint-Simon and Saint-Simonism* (London, Longmans, Green, Reader, and Dyer, 1871), pp. 119-120, for circumstances leading to the change. H. J. Hunt, *Le Socialisme et le romantisme en France: Étude de la presse socialiste de 1830 à 1848* (Oxford, Clarendon Press, 1935), p. 47, dates the change November 11th.] On January 18, 1831, the subtitle changed to *Journal de la doctrine de Saint-Simon*. On January 1, 1832, the subtitle again changed to *Journal de la religion de Saint-Simonienne*. And on April 20, 1832, the periodical ceased publication. References are to a microphotographic reproduction of the file at Bibliothèque Nationale, Paris.)

" La révolution de 1789 avait déraciné, sur le sol de la France, l'ordre féodal, déjà privé de sève, desséché, foudroyé par Louis XIV." (*Le Globe*, 7th year, no. 38 [February 7, 1831], p. 149. The article is by Laurent.)

". . . la révolution française devait commencer par détruire radicalement l'ordre social fondé sur le catholicisme et la féodalité . . . ." (*L'Organisateur*, 2nd year, no. 29 [March 5, 1831], p. 222.)

France is the only large monarchy in Europe in which the social revolution, operating gradually during several centuries, has been definitely completed by a violent crisis. The crisis, the French Revolution, is a " vaste ébranlement "; a study of it and its causes shows " la société théologique-féodale dans les phases diverses de son agonie." (*Le Producteur*, IV, 470. The article is by Laurent.)

Feudalism is annihilated. (*L'Industrie*, as reprinted in *Oeuvres*, XIX, 53.)

[27] " Les écrivains de second ordre qui se sont traînés sur les pas de

doctrines of liberty and individualism are the negation of all other social doctrines.[28]

(5) Interpretation of the Present and the Future in the Light of Periodicity.

In the Nineteenth Century, destruction is no longer necessary.[29] The task of the present [c. 1830] is con-

Montesquieu et du misanthrope de Genève n'ont fait que commenter et paraphraser leurs maîtres; ils ont attaqué en détail, et démoli pièce à pièce l'édifice du passé, et quand leur tâche a été complètement consommé, en 1793, ils ont montré au monde leur impuissance pour reconstruire sur des bases nouvelles." (*Exposition*, 1st year, 8th séance, p. 303.)

Liberty of conscience, such at least as it has been in the past, is not an end: "née pour détruire, elle ne se maintient encore aujourd'hui que par opposition à de faux systèmes; à cet égard, elle ne fait que constater un fait, l'absence d'une doctrine en harmonie avec les besoins de la société. La prolongation de ce principe ne serait donc que celle de l'anarchie dont nous nous plaignons." (*Le Producteur*, I, 412. The article is by Bazard.)

". . . le dogme de la souvéraineté populaire n'a aucune valeur d'organisation, et . . . il n'a été bon qu'à démolir le passé . . . ." (*Le Globe*, 7th year, no. 105 [April 15, 1831], p. 421.)

Liberalism can do nothing to ameliorate the lot of the class that is poorest and most numerous; that aim was foreign to its sympathies and theories. (*L'Organisateur*, apparently no. 51, as reprinted in *Oeuvres*, II, 235.)

Criticism can never hope to destroy completely the institutions of the past. (*Ibid.*, II, 236.)

Representative government is "l'institution bâtarde." (*Ibid.*, II, 238.)

[28] "Les hommes de la *critique* n'avaient pas remarqué que tous leurs dogmes n'avaient qu'une valeur *négative*; que chacun d'eux était purement et simplement la *négation* d'un dogme ou d'un principe constitutif correspondant du système catholique et féodal; que tous se résumaient dans l'*égoisme*, l'individualisme, qui est la *négation* d'un ordre social quelconque. Ils ont cru et ils ont proclamé que ces principes étaient des vérités éternelles, immuables, qui devaient être appliqués en tout temps et en tout lieu; qu'ils étaient la base sur laquelle il fallait appuyer une organisation sociale définitive. En cela, ils se sont doublement trompés." (*L'Organisateur*, 2nd year, no. 31 [March 19, 1831], p. 241.)

". . . la doctrine de la liberté, qui n'est pas autre chose que la négation de toute doctrine sociale. (*Le Producteur*, IV, 388. The article is by Enfantin.)

[29] "Le XVIIIe siècle n'a fait que détruire; nous ne continuerons point

structively to prepare the organization of the new sys-

son ouvrage: ce que nous entreprenons, au contraire, c'est de jeter les fondements d'une construction nouvelle . . . . " (*L'Industrie,* April, 1817, as reprinted in *Oeuvres,* XVIII, 13.)

" . . . si l'oeuvre du dix-huitième siècle n'était pas accomplie nous la continuerions avec ardeur; nous serions les premiers à combattre le passé; les premiers, nous voudrions en finir à jamais avec le moyen âge. Mais le Catholicisme est expirant, Voltaire a passé par là; la féodalité est vaincue à jamais, 93 nous en sépare: . . . laissant donc le libéralisme balayer sans effort ces ruines, enterrer en un jour ces cadavres, nous croyons devoir nous consacrer à une oeuvre plus grande, à élever un nouvel edifice *religieux,* c'est-à-dire, si nous nous sommes bien fait comprendre, un nouvel édifice *social.* On voit que notre oeuvre n'est pas opposée à celle des *libéraux;* elle en est la suite, le complément nécessaire, le superbe couronnement." (*Le Globe,* 7th year, no. 361 [December 27, 1831], p. 1440.)

" Vous [the liberals] aviez mission de détruire une organisation odieuse, d'effacer des privilèges héréditaires détestés . . . . Gloire à vous, libéraux! votre tâche était gigantesque et votre dévouement a été colossal . . . ." But, the destructive task having been done, the liberals are urged to unite with the Saint-Simonians to free the laborers. (*Ibid.,* 7th year, no. 33 [February 2, 1831], p. 129. A similar statement occurs in issue 51 [February 20, 1831], p. 201.

" Depuis les événements de juillet, nous l'avons déjà dit, la mission intérieure du liberalisme est achevée . . . ." (*Ibid.,* 7th year, no. 70 [March 11, 1831], p. 279.)

" Messieurs, nous sommes en révolution; la révolution française dure encore, car son but n'est pas atteint." The French Revolution was a reaction,—the destruction of an old system. Thus far, there have been three attempts at reorganization. (1) The Convention abolished feudalism and the Catholic Church; but, in insisting upon the equality of all men, it ignored " la véritable Loi Naturelle, la véritable condition du *progrès social,* l'inégalité." (2) During the Empire, Napoleon had no more power than the Convention had had to institute a definitive social order; his mission was to stop destruction in France, to propagate revolution in Europe, and to restore to France consciousness of its own force. (3) The Restoration, though it was a less retrograde attempt than either of the other two, failed also. (*Ibid.,* 7th year, no. 195 [July 14, 1831], p. 784.)

The aim of the French Revolution is not yet completed; therefore we are still in revolution. The aim of the Revolution was the definitive emancipation of humanity, the substitution of a common law for the privileges of the ancient law, and the consecration of the rights of man. " Partant la révolution française devait commencer par détruire radicalement l'ordre social fondé sur le catholicisme et la féodalité; elle ne pourra *finir* que par l'institution d'une société fondée sur des principes différents

tem, which is to rise out of the ruins of the old one.[30]

de ceux qui ont servi de base aux sociétés du passé." (*L'Organisateur,* 2nd year, no. 29 [March 5, 1831], p. 222.)

"Mais pour atteindre ce but magnifique, il ne faut pas se borner à la *propagande révolutionnaire*; il faut aussi (et c'est là surtout la partie la plus importante de la mission de la France), il faut songer à la PROPAGANDE ORGANISATRICE. Quand vous aurez fait un vide immense sur le débris de l'Europe féodale et chrétienne par la philosophie et par les armes, pourrez-vous laisser longtemps sans abri les peuples que vous aurez excités à la démolition de l'antique masure qui leur servait de refuge? Non, il sera instant d'élever un nouvel édifice, et ce sera pour lors le tour de L'INTERVENTION PACIFIQUE, de l'INTERVENTION RELIGIEUSE . . . ." (*Le Globe,* 7th year, no. 38 [February 7, 1831], p. 149.)

[30] See *ante, Note 29.*

Also, "La génération actuelle est appelée à préparer l'organisation du nouveau système. . . . Nous essayons d'indiquer aux savants, aux industriels et aux artistes, comment ils doivent combiner leurs connaissances et leurs sentiments dans l'intérêt de l'utilité commune, de leur gloire particulière et de leur propre dignité." (*Le Producteur,* I, 9. The article is by A. Cerclet.)

We are today in a critical epoch "au sein de laquelle s'élabore l'époque organique définitive." (*L'Organisateur,* 1st year, no. 20 [December 27, 1829], p. 3.)

After commenting on and characterizing the last critical era, a writer in *Le Globe* says: The man of genius, no longer able to live among the ruins of a dead society, raises himself out of the abyss. (*Le Globe,* 7th year, no. 361 [December 27, 1831], p. 1440.)

". . . il est nécessaire de reconstruire le nouvel édifice spirituel de la société dont les matériaux sont épars . . . ." (*La Producteur,* III, 12. The article is by Enfantin.)

". . . examinez seulement si la marche du passé ne nous annonce pas une réconciliation prochaine entre les génies de ces grands hommes . . . . Voyez . . . si nous ne sommes pas (suivant l'expression de M BALLANCHE) à la fin d'une de ces crises *palingénésiques* où s'opère le passage d'une époque critique épuisée, à une époque organique nouvelle, c'est-à-dire où la société, fatiguée de vivre sans lien moral, sait en découvrir un nouveau, plus fort que celui qui a été détruit, et auquel la critique elle-même consent peu à peu à se soumettre." (*Exposition,* 1st year, 14th séance, p. 433.)

"Au milieu de cette [old] société qui tombe en ruines, une autre société s'élève pleine de jeunesse et de vigueur; là chacun est *placé selon sa capacité et récompensé selon ses oeuvres*; là on obéit avec amour, car c'est avec amour qu'on commande; là on marche avec une science certaine vers un but certain." (*L'Organisateur* [probably no. 51] as reprinted in *Oeuvres,* II, 244. The article is by Bazard and Enfantin together.)

Saint-Simon himself realized "que ce n'est pas à nous qu'il est réservé

The golden age lies in the future.[31] In preparing the organization of the future society the general law of perfectibility must be kept in mind.[32] Humanity is not to be bound in absolute and unchangeable forms without room for adjustment of theory to practice.[32] But the main features of the future organization can be outlined in advance.[32] The disorder and anarchy that have

d'instituer le régime industriel; mais que nous devons en préparer l'établissement par de grands travaux philosophiques, dont nous avons indiqué plus haut la nature et la nécessité . . . ." (*L'Industrie*, III, 1817, as reprinted in *Oeuvres*, XIX, 31.)

[31] Saint-Simon's statement " L'âge d'or, qu'une aveugle tradition a placé jusqu'ici dans le passé, est devant nous " is quoted frequently by the Saint-Simonians. For example, it is the motto used on the title-page of *Le Producteur*. And in *Le Producteur*, I, 440, Carrel assigns the motto to Saint-Simon.

[32] " Nous ne vous tracerons cependant qu'à grands traits, car nous craindrions d'être infidèles à la loi de la perfectibilité humaine, si nous ne laissions aux générations qui nous succéderont le soin d'améliorer une foule de détails plus ou moins importants et que nous ne pouvons entrevoir que d'une manière imparfaite.—Nous ne voulons point d'ailleurs imprisonner l'humanité dans des formes *absolues, invariables*; nous savons que la *pratique* viendra souvent rectifier les données de la *theorie*." (*Le Globe*, 7th year, no. 259 [September 16, 1831], p. 1036.)

The Saint-Simonian doctrine is not an absolute system or order of things. Instead, it is a doctrine of opportunism. (*Ibid.*, 7th year, no. 196 [July 15, 1831], p. 785.)

The passages just cited from *Le Globe*, which are expressions of the basic Saint-Simonian belief in indefinite (instead of attainable) perfectibility of man, should prevent misunderstanding of the Saint-Simonians' statements that the future organic epoch will be a definitive state. For example, a statement that might easily be misunderstood occurs in *Exposition*, 1st year (4th séance, p. 206). The lecture says: From a standpoint that includes the total duration of the life of humanity on earth, " la société comprend deux états généraux distincts: l'un provisoire, qui appartient au passé, l'autre définitif, qui est réservé à l'avenir . . . ." But obviously that statement about a *definitive state* does not mean a state of affairs in which progress and change will be suspended. For the preceding lecture (*Exposition*, 1st year, 3rd séance, p. 200) had been more specific when it said: Humanity is moving toward a definitive state, in which progress can operate without interruption; " nous marchons vers un monde où la religion et la philosophie, le culte et les beaux-arts, le dogme et la science, ne seront plus divisés . . . ."

arisen in society must give way to a new centralized hierarchic order.[33] The analytic philosophy that reigns in divisive eras must be subordinated to a new directive synthesis of religion, polity, science, and beaux-arts.[34] The constitutive element, or unifying bond, in the new order will be religion.[35] And this new encyclopaedic

[33] Enfantin's letter to the Saint-Simonians during the July Revolution speaks of the old disorder and anarchy, and calls the new order "la hiérarchie nouvelle." (*L'Organisateur,* August 1, 1830, as reprinted in *Oeuvres,* II, 214.)

An article entitled "L'Ordre Légal" conceives of society as an hierarchy and uses the term "la hiérarchie sociale." (*Le Globe,* 7th year, no. 188 [July 7, 1831].)

". . . hiéarchie sociale" in the future. (*Ibid.,* 7th year, no. 252 [September 9, 1831], p. 1005.)

"La *centralisation* . . . est corrélative de civilisation, d'harmonie, d'edification." (*Ibid.,* 7th year, no. 202 [July 21, 1831], p. 809.)

"Mais, pour que cette association [i. e., association industrielle] soit réalisée et produise tous ses fruits, il faut qu'elle constitue une hiérarchie, il faut qu'une vue générale préside à ses travaux et les harmonise." (*Exposition,* 2nd year, 1st séance [*Oeuvres,* XLII, 164-165].)

". . . pour nous, toute SOCIÉTÉ véritable est une HIÉRARCHIE." (*Ibid.,* 2nd year, 9th séance [*Oeuvres,* XLII, 326]. However, there is no positive proof that Carlyle read this 9th lecture: see *ante,* note 2.)

[34] A writer in *Le Globe* (some M. A . . .) insists that the last critical epoch will be followed by an organic epoch and comments upon a religious synthesis as superior to the analytic philosophy that reigns in divisive epochs, that stresses individualism, that does not see beyond details, and that does not recognize the necessity of a synthetic view (*lien*). (*Le Globe,* 7th year, no. 361 [December 27, 1831], p. 1440.)

". . . nous marchons vers un monde où la religion et la philosophie, le culte et les beaux-arts, le dogme et la science, ne seront plus divisés . . . ." (*Exposition,* 1st year, 3rd séance, p. 200.)

". . . si la science est aujourd'hui athée, nous ne devons attribuer ce fait qu'à l'époque critique dans laquelle nous sommes; époque qui, s'il faut en croire l'expérience du passé, nous annonce l'apparition prochaine d'un état social dans lequel la science reprendra le caractère religieux qu'elle a toujours eu dans les époques organiques." (*Exposition,* 1st year, 14th séance, pp. 440-441.)

The first article in the first issue of *L'Organisateur* has as its title "De la nécessité d'une nouvelle doctrine générale." (*L'Organisateur,* 1st year, no. 1 [August 15, 1829], p. 1.)

[35] ". . . l'élément constitutif, . . la raison suprême de toute société,

synthesis must fit the needs of humanity, must harmonize the new factual discoveries, and must be credible as a whole and in its parts.[36]

[est] la RELIGION . . . . " (*Exposition,* 2nd year, 3rd séance [*Oeuvres,* XLII, 194].)

". . . l'essence d'une *religion* c'est de *relier* les hommes entre eux. Une société n'est religieuse qu'autant que ses membres sont animés de pensées communes, d'une même volonté; qu'autant que les sentiments généraux sont superposés à *l'égoïsme* ou fondus avec lui. Dès lors vous devez sentir comme nous que le seul remède aux maux qui dévorent la société, le seul baume qui puisse adoucir et cicatriser ses plaies continuelles, c'est un *nouveau lien,* une *religion nouvelle.*" (*L'Organisateur,* 2nd year, no. 28 [February 26, 1831], p. 221.)

". . . l'HUMANITÉ A UN AVENIR RELIGIEUX;—la *religion de l'avenir sera plus grande, plus puissante, qu'aucune des religions du passé; son dogme sera la synthèse de toutes les conceptions, de toutes les manières d'être de l'homme;*— l'INSTITUTION SOCIALE, POLITIQUE, CONSIDÉRÉE DANS SON ENSEMBLE, SERA UNE INSTITUTION RELIGIEUSE." (*Exposition,* 2nd year, 1st séance [*Oeuvres,* XLII, 172-173]. Here, as heretofore, the italics and the capitals are in the text. The last word in the passage just quoted is printed in letters twice the size of ordinary capitals.)

[36] See *ante, Note 33,* as well as the following passages from *Le Producteur.*

In the positive industrial scheme each maxim will be demonstrable,—having been built on knowledge of social phenomena. The foundation of the whole is the principle of progressive modification of systems to keep step with the ascending progress of the human spirit. Therefore faith is not asked to accept something like the old dogmatism. Instead, " l'examen, si redoubtable pour ce dernier, devenu l'auxiliaire de la foi, dans l'ordre scientifique industriel, où la doctrine devra toujours être l'expression des idées et des besoins contemporains, ne pourra que changer des *croyans par confiance, en croyans par démonstration,* et favoriser le perfectionnement continu que la nouvelle école a précisément pour but d'accélérer et d'étendre le plus possible." (*Le Producteur,* II, 541. The writer of the article is P. M. L. [i. e., Laurent].)

" Tous les anciens dogmes religieux sont, au fond, une transformation sentimentale des premiers aperçus scientifiques de l'humanité, la religion considérée positivement, est une science d'application qui sert d'intermédiaire entre les savans et le peuple, et de base à l'enseignement moral." (*Ibid.,* III, 296. The writer of the article is O. R. [i. e., Olinde Rodrigues].)

" Il faut refaire le catéchisme, le livre élémentaire par excellence, pour le mettre en harmonie avec les progrès de l'esprit humain . . . ." Though the old catechism is of no value as truth, it should be kept until it can be advantageously replaced. The new catechisms will have to be a great

That much just given must suffice for the Saint-Simonian concept of periodicity in history:—made up of their law of progressive periodic mutation, their characterizations of the two alternate epochs, their notion of transition between periods, their tracing of two complete periods in past European history, and their interpretation of the present and the future in the light of periodicity. It obviously verges over at the end into a social philosophy. And we must stop short there. It was that philosophy of history, with those special points, that Carlyle came in contact with in 1830 and 1831 in the writings of the Saint-Simonians.

condensation, on an encyclopaedic organization, of positive philosophy. A good catechism can be made only after a good encyclopaedia—a coordination and linking-together of full human knowledge—has been made. (*Ibid.*, III, 302-303. This passage is from Rodrigues' article just quoted above.)

CHAPTER III

The First Year of Carlyle's Contact with Saint-Simonian Thought (1830-1831)

The evidence on Carlyle's relations with the Saint-Simonians from the beginning until his visit to London in 1831 is found chiefly in the letters and journals. Although during many of those months he was occupied with the production of *Sartor Resartus*, the evidence from *Sartor* may properly be reserved until the next chapter, which will begin with an examination of that first major work completed under the Saint-Simonian influence. Meanwhile, the present chapter will examine the circumstances under which the first direct contacts with the Society were made, the list of important writings by Saint-Simon and the Saint-Simonian Society that Carlyle is known to have read before August 1831, and the reactions that he recorded in his letters and journal up until about two months before the completion of *Sartor*.

The steps by which Carlyle came into contact with Saint-Simonian thought in 1830 and 1831 throw light upon the problem of influence. The first step in the *rapprochement* between the French socialists and the Scotch reviewer was occasioned by the unconscious and unelaborated similarities between Carlyle's thought in " Signs of the Times " and the Saint-Simonian view on social conditions. Impressed by the reproduction of " Signs of the Times " in *Revue britannique* [1] the Saint-

[1] The November issue, 1829, pp. 3-29. See A. C. Taylor's *Carlyle et la pensée latine*, p. 25.

<50></50>

Simonians used their weekly *L'Organisateur* in the spring of 1830 to publish a critique of Carlyle's essay.[2] Though Laurent, the writer of the Saint-Simonian critique, followed *Revue britannique* in attributing the unsigned *Edinburgh Review* article to Sydney Smith, Laurent on his own responsibility called the author of " Signs " " le sage critique " and called the " Signs " itself " un article extrêmement remarquable." [3] By digests and quotations, Laurent undertook to point out to readers of *L'Organisateur* what he considered the most salient passages in " Signs of the Times,"

qui reproduit la plupart de nos jugemens sur l'époque actuelle, en nous réservant d'ajouter à cette citation quelques réflexions sur les lacunes ou les erreurs que renferme le travail de l'illustre Anglais, et qui ne sont guère aperceptibles que du point de vue Saint-Simonien.[4]

From the French critique it is clear that Laurent understood and appreciated the British writer's use of irony.[5] He heartily approved, and believed strikingly true, the Briton's indictment of the mechanistic tendencies prevalent in all phases of life in the age.[6] But he regretfully noted what he believed a tendency of that writer himself to leave the solution of social problems to pure economics.[7] He deplored the writer's prescription to fecundate genius by isolating it, and lamented the writer's blindness to the beneficial effects of association and unity.[8]

[2] *L'Organisateur* divided P. M. Laurent's critique of " Signs " into two parts: the first part appeared in *L'Organisateur*, 1st year, no. 32 (March 21, 1830), pp. 2-4; the second part, in no. 36 (April 18), pp. 2-3.

[3] *Ibid.*, 1st year, no. 32 (March 21, 1830), pp. 3 and 2.

[4] *Ibid.*, 1st year, no. 32 (March 21, 1830), p. 2.

[5] *Ibid.*, 1st year, no. 36 (April 18, 1830), p. 2.

[6] *Ibid.*, 1st year, no. 32 (March 21, 1830), pp. 3-4 and no. 36 (April 18, 1830), p. 2.

[7] *Ibid.*, 1st year, no. 32 (March 21, 1830), pp. 2-3.

[8] *Ibid.*, 1st year, no. 36 (April 18, 1830), p. 3.

Mais pour que les résultats les plus merveilleux de la médi-
tation solitaire ne restent pas stériles, il est indispensable
qu'ils sortent de l'obscurité, et leur fructification est alors
d'autant plus abondante qu'elle devient l'objet d'une plus
grande combinaison d'efforts.[9]

Having thus pointed out some community of viewpoint—as well as some differences—between themselves
and Carlyle, and being desirous of making proselytes to
their cause in Britain, the Saint-Simonian Society proceeded to the next step in July 1830. Apparently before
mid-July, Gustave d'Eichthal, acting for the Society,
despatched to the author of " Signs of the Times " a
packet of Saint-Simonian publications accompanied by
a letter. The packet of course included issues of *L'Organisateur*. Only three issues of the periodical were
referred to specifically: Numbers 32 and 36, containing
the critique on " Signs of the Times," and Number 34,
containing an explanatory comment on Saint-Simon's
Nouveau Christianisme.[10] But from the later directions
in the letter, it is certain that quite a few other issues
were included in the packet. And in the same packet
containing the various issues of *L'Organisateur*, d'Eichthal included five other publications: *Nouveau Christianisme, Aux Artistes, Le Producteur, L'Industrie*, and
Eugène Rodrigues' translation of Lessing's *L'Education
du genre humain*.[11] Hoping to facilitate understanding
of the documents, the Saint-Simonian apostle gave some
helpful directions concerning the various works and the
order in which they should be read. That is, he wished
the author of " Signs of the Times " to begin by reading the two articles concerning his own essay, and then

[9] *Ibid.*
[10] Eugène d'Eichthal, " Carlyle et la Saint-Simonisme," *Revue historique*, LXXXII (1903), 292-293.
[11] For bibliographical data on the six publications, see footnotes in
Chapter II.

to go to the explanatory comment on *Nouveau Chris-tianisme.* The next item in the sequence was to be *Nouveau Christianisme* itself. He was then to proceed with the numbers of *L'Organisateur* containing exposi-tions of the principal points of Saint-Simonian dogma that had been presented in the public seances during the year.[12] And after reading the expository seances, he was to turn to *Aux Artistes.*[13]

Those first communications from the Saint-Simonians reached Carlyle near the end of July.[14] They came as a surprise. The praise, both expressed and implied in the published critique and in the private letter, had been directed to the author of " Signs of the Times " by a group of strangers in France, as recognition of the worth of his work. And to Carlyle in the late summer of 1830, such offerings of recognition and praise were sweet water in the desert. Isolation at Craigenputtock, literary ob-scurity, and financial poverty, oppressive as they had long been, had just been aggravated by the death of his favorite sister and by the collapse of the project of German literary history, on which his energies had been at a stretch for many months. Under such circum-stances, Carlyle could feel to the quick the truth in Laurent's comment on the sterilizing effects of soli-tude.[15] Since this study cannot examine Carlyle's points

[12] From Gustave d'Eichthal's letter it is impossible to say how many of the thirteen seances later to be published in the *Exposition*, 2nd year, were included in the packet.

[13] For all these valuable directions concerning the order in which the items were to be read, see *Revue historique*, LXXXII (1903), 293.

[14] *The Letters of Thomas Carlyle (1826-1836)*, edited by C. E. Norton (London, 1889), p. 166. (This letter to Carlyle's mother was written apparently about August 3, 1830.) See also *ibid.*, p. 168; *Revue his-torique*, LXXXII (1903), 294; *Two Note Books,* p. 158; and *Correspond-ence between Goethe and Carlyle,* p. 214.

[15] See, for example, J. A. Froude, *Thomas Carlyle . . . 1795-1835* (New York, Scribner's, 1882), II, 96 and 98, and *Two Note Books,* pp. 163-165.

of sympathy with the Saint-Simonian social teachings, it must suffice to note here that Carlyle's letters within the next few weeks show his heart warmed by d'Eichthal's offer of intellectual association with a group of brilliant and cultivated men of another nation, far enough advanced in their viewpoint to be to some extent like-minded with himself. Finally, the chief circumstance making the time particularly auspicious for the arrival of the tactfully introduced Saint-Simonian publications and for the beginning of a Saint-Simonian influence must be stressed. Through hardships and discouragements, Carlyle had for many months groped his way toward some plan of historical evolution by periodic movements. So much the more ready was he to appreciate the fine Saint-Simonian concept of periodicity when, late in 1830 and in 1831, he found an exposition of it ready-formed, worked out, and perfectly fusible with, and supplementary to, his earlier influences and his own painful advances beyond those early influences.

Some three weeks after the arrival of the packet out of France, Carlyle wrote, August 9th, to d'Eichthal, acknowledging receipt of the letter and the various publications—all in good condition. He had already looked over the writings in the order that d'Eichthal had indicated. He had been more favorably impressed by the writings of the disciples than by those of the master. And he intended to investigate the Society and its doctrine further when the opportunity offered. Already he had found much to approve.

In these Books of your Society, which for most part were new to me, I find little or nothing to dissent from: the spirit at least meets my entire sympathy; the opinions also are often such as I, in my own dialect, have been accustomed to cherish, and more or less clearly enunciate.[16]

---

[16] In a paragraph after the signature, Carlyle adds the following sug-

That the last century was a period of Denial, of Irreligion and Destruction; to which a new period of Affirmation, of Religion, must succeed, if Society is to be reconstituted, or even to continue in existence: this with its thousand corollaries is a proposition for which the thinking minds of all nations are prepared.[17]

The last sentence of the passage just quoted is as close as Carlyle came, in this August letter, to a comment on the Saint-Simonian concept of periodicity. He was also interested, it should be noted, in the social aspects of the Saint-Simonian writings. And he was greatly interested in religion. Though he admitted that, for the present, no public religion existed, he was confident that, in the future, one must—and would—exist, for he regarded religion as the basis of society. But he doubted that the religion of the future would be the New Christianity of Saint-Simon. Thus frankly doubting, he nevertheless asked for further information on the religious phase of the Society's doctrine—specifically, on how " scientific insight has transformed itself into Religion." [18] Indeed, he was much interested in all facts concerning the Society:

. . . the whole history and actual constitution of your Society, its aspects internal and external, its numbers, its political and economical relations, its whole manner of being and acting, are questions of unusual interest for me.[19]

gestion: " Some clearer insight, into my views, moral and Religious, which as originating from almost the opposite point of vision, yet curiously corresponding, your society might find it interesting to compare with their own, is to be had in an Article entitled *Voltaire,* No. 6 of *Foreign Review*; in *Novalis,* No. 7 of the same periodical, and *Goethe,* No. 3 the *Foreign Review* . . . . ' " " Carlyle's Letters to the Socialists of 1830," *The New Quarterly* (London, Dent, 1909), II, 277-288, seems to be Carlyle's own diction, whereas the earlier *Revue historique* (1903), pp. 292-306, version is a translation.

[17] *The New Quarterly,* II (1909), 280.
[18] *Ibid.,* II, 281.
[19] *Ibid.,* II, 282.

And the letter closed thus:

. . . heartily wishing you good speed, nay, in my own place and way, striving to work together with you, I remain,

My Dear Sir,
Your and your Society's friend and servant,
Thomas Carlyle.[20]

During the rest of 1830, Carlyle did find—and make—opportunities to investigate the Saint-Simonians further. For example, about a week after the letter just quoted, a notebook entry comments thus on the Society:

These people have strange notions, not without a large spicing of truth, and are themselves among the *Signs.* I feel curious to know what becomes of them. . . . I answered these *St. Ss.* and partly expect to hear from them again.[21]

A letter to John Carlyle only a few days later is worth noting too, fusing, as it does, thoughts about history and thoughts about society. It comments that the wretched social conditions—more wretched than they have been since the time of Nero and Christ—are rising to a head and will some day blow up. And, Carlyle adds,

the gig, and gigmania must rot or start into thousand shivers, and bury itself in the ditch, that *Man* may have clean roadway towards the goal whither through all ages he is tending. *Fiat, fiat!* [22]

This passage, comparing the present era to First Century Rome and insisting that the present social organization will and should destroy itself, is in line with

---

[20] *Ibid.,* II, 283.
[21] *Two Note Books,* p. 158.
[22] J. A. Froude, *Thomas Carlyle . . . 1795-1835,* II, 97-98. The letter to John Carlyle is dated August 21st.

Saint-Simonian thought concerning recurrent critical eras, in which the worn-out social systems disintegrate.[23] Obviously puzzled by the Saint-Simonians and their writings, Carlyle asked Goethe's opinion upon them.[24] And Goethe's warning words came back late in the fall: " Von der Société St. Simonienne bitte Sich fern zu halten." [25] Goethe's reply found Carlyle already engaged on the piece " On Clothes," [26] which was ultimately to grow, with the aid of the Saint-Simonians, into *Sartor*. Writing to his brother John, November 12th, Carlyle repeated Goethe's warning against the Society, but added: " Nevertheless, send me their Books by the very first chance." [27] And John immediately promised to send, early in December, something that he designated as the " Simonienne." [28] Apparently Car-

[23] For related statements on social conditions, see *Two Note Books,* pp. 178-79 (between November 24 and December 29, 1830); and *Correspondence between Goethe and Carlyle,* p. 259 (January 22, 1831).

[24] *Ibid.,* pp. 214-215.

[25] *Ibid.,* p. 225. Goethe's letter was dated October 17, 1830. His warning was memorable, and Carlyle kept it in mind enough to repeat it several times in German or in English. It is interesting to read Soret's record of Goethe's question and comment on October 20, 1830, concerning the Saint-Simonians (J. P. Eckermann, *Gespräche mit Goethe in den letzten Jahren seines Lebens* [ed. by Conrad Höfer, Leipzig, Hesse und Becker, 1913], pp. 702-703.

[26] *Two Note Books,* p. 177 (October 28, 1830): " Written a strange piece ' On Clothes ': know not what will come of it."

[27] *Letters of Thomas Carlyle, 1826-1836,* p. 176.

[28] John Carlyle's letter, postmarked November 15th and presumably still in manuscript in the Pierpont Morgan Library, has been seen by Professor Neff (*Carlyle,* pp. 120 and 274). Professor Neff explains thus the term " Simonienne ": " probably the collection in book form of the lectures printed in the *Organisateur.*" He obviously means *Exposition de la Doctrine Saint-Simonienne, Deuxième Année,* which was published as a book in December 1830. I believe the more probable significance of John's term " Simonienne," when associated with Carlyle's request for " Books " (in the plural), is the *Doctrine de Saint-Simon, Exposition Première Année* (pub. August 1830), and the rest of the contents of the second package of Saint-Simonian publications. Carlyle had certainly received this second packet by January 22, 1831 (see *Correspondence*

lyle's hurry in connection with the Saint-Simonian books was occasioned by his activities in translating *Nouveau Christianisme* and preparing an Introduction to go with the translation. The translation and short Introduction were finished by December 19th, with the view of sending the work to London for his brother to dispose of to any publisher, for cash.[29] This " heterodox Pamphlet," as Carlyle called it, " contains several strange ideas, not without a large spice of truth; is ill-written, but easily read, and deserves a reading." [30] Thus, by the end of 1830, though Carlyle had known the Saint-Simonian Society, at first hand, only five months, he had already read with interest and with some approval a considerable number of their publications, had begun his correspondence with one of the apostles, and had translated the last work produced by the master and had written an Introduction to it.

At some time near the end of the old year or near the beginning of the new, Carlyle received a second packet of Saint-Simonian documents from Paris. On January 22, 1831, in a letter to Goethe he specified the contents

between *Goethe and Carlyle*, p. 258, and *The New Quarterly*, II, 283). Carlyle's first letter to d'Eichthal had given, in addition to his address in Scotland, the name of Black, Young, and Young as London publishers with whom he had connections. (*Revue historique*, LXXXII [1903], 297. The *New Quarterly* version of that letter omits the passage about the London publishing firm.) Presumably Carlyle had mentioned this connection with the London publishing firm in order to suggest to d'Eichthal a cheap conveyance of future book-packets from Paris. It therefore seems logical that in the letter to John on November 12th—" Nevertheless, send me their Books by the very first chance "—Carlyle was asking his brother to forward the new Saint-Simonian book-packet from the Black storeroom by the first conveyance to Scotland. Presumably Carlyle had already examined in *L'Organisateur* many of the seances of the *Exposition, Deuxième Année*. And the terms " Books " in Carlyle's letter and the " Simonienne " in John's letter would fit a packet of Saint-Simonian publications better than they would fit one single volume.

[29] *Letters of Thomas Carlyle, 1826-1836*, p. 178.
[30] *Ibid.*

of this packet as "a large mass of their performances: Expositions of their Doctrine;[31] Proclamations sent forth during the famous Three Days;[32] many numbers of their weekly Journal."[33] And to Goethe, who had recently warned him against this French Society, he added the following comment.

They seem to me to be earnest, zealous, and nowise ignorant men, but wandering in strange paths. I should say they have discovered and laid to heart this momentous and now almost forgotten truth, *Man is still Man*; and are already beginning to make false applications of it.[34] I have every disposition to follow your advice, and stand apart from them; looking on their Society and its progress nevertheless as a true and remarkable Sign of the Times.[35]

If, by the time Carlyle received this second packet of the Society's publications, he had decided to follow Goethe's advice and to stand apart from the Society, he had not decided to ignore their thought. And the delay of several months before he wrote d'Eichthal acknowledging receipt of this second installment may have been occasioned by the fact that he was still undecided about their thought or by the fact that he was busy adjusting

[31] *I. e., Doctrine de Saint-Simon, Exposition première année,* Paris, 1830. See letter of May 17, 1831, *Revue historique,* LXXXII, 298, and *The New Quarterly,* II, 283. See also *Revue historique,* LXXXII, 297, where Eugène d'Eichthal says that his father, after August 9, 1830, sent Carlyle a book.

[32] Carlyle probably has in mind, for one thing, the proclamation signed by Bazard and Enfantin and posted in Paris July 30, 1830: *Oeuvres de Saint-Simon et d'Enfantin,* II, 198-200; see also II, 191. A year after its first appearance, this proclamation was reprinted in *Le Globe,* no. 213, 7th year (August 1, 1831), pp. 854-855.

[33] *I. e., L'Organisateur, Journal de la doctrine de Saint-Simon.* See also *Revue historique,* LXXXII, 298, or *The New Quarterly,* II, 283.

[34] Norton (*Correspondence between Goethe and Carlyle,* p. 258, footnote) points out the close resemblance between this estimate and the one in *Sartor Resartus,* Book III, chapter xii.

[35] *Correspondence between Goethe and Carlyle,* pp. 258-259.

his own thought to some of the Saint-Simonian tenets, which he was to incorporate into his own writings. At all events, his notebook entry of February 7th shows his continued interest in the Society: " Could write . . . a Paper on the Saint-Simonians." [36]

Two essays on the history of German literature, finished during the winter and spring of 1831, deserve attention here. In them, Carlyle reworked some of the material from his unfinished book on the history of German literature. The fact that part of the material in the essays thus dates from early 1830 and part from 1831 makes it impossible to assign definite Saint-Simonian influence to any part. Neither essay contains any specific allusion to the Saint-Simonians. But, for the sake of completeness, the evidence on historical periodicity should be noted.

The first of the two essays, finished by January 20, 1831, dealt with Taylor's *Historic Survey of German Poetry*. The evidence on historical periodicity can be re-stated as follows. Human progress proceeds through alternate phases of growth and decay. Man cannot stand still or retrograde; from every moral death, there is a new birth.[37] A literary historian must discover the grand spiritual tendency of each period and show how one epoch naturally evolved itself out of its predecessor.[38] A study of German literary history reveals an alternation of poetic and didactic eras. After the German nation had struggled out of paganism and the chaos of the Northern Immigrations had gradually settled, there developed a new and fairer world. At length, in the Swabian era, arose a blaze of simple but true poetry. To that first poetic era—the Swabian—succeeded an era of inquiry or didacticism. That didac-

[36] *Two Note Books*, p. 183.   [37] *Essays*, II, 345.   [38] *Ibid.*, II, 342.

ticism reached a poetic acme under Luther. After Luther, the prosaic character resumed sway. Inquiry and criticism pushed beyond their proper limits; and understanding alone was listened to.[39] But under Lessing and Klopstock, Germany roused again and shook off its fetters.[40] The epoch that followed Lessing and Klopstock has deep significance, for the want of the age in all Europe then took voice and shape in Germany. The change from negation to affirmation, destruction to re-construction, is perhaps now in action in Germany. In German literature, some say, lie the rudiments of a new spiritual age, for this age and later ones to work out.[41] How long the present European democracy or anarchy will last is a subject for conjecture. But we do see and know that there is a tendency toward a universal European commonweal. Europe is to have its true Sacred College and Council of Amphictyons. And wars are to become rarer and possibly obsolete.[42]

Thus Carlyle's essay on Taylor's *Historic Survey* shows a concept of periodicity in history made up of alternate epochs of poetry and didacticism. In applying that concept, Carlyle singled out the Twelfth, the Sixteenth, and the late Eighteenth and early Nineteenth Centuries as three poetic epochs, separated from each other by didactic epochs. Of course his material offered him no opportunity to apply the concept of periodicity to earlier eras, of classical culture. Commenting upon the present, Carlyle finds in contemporary German literature the want of the age: the change from negation to affirmation, possibly the rudiments of a new spiritual era. And in spite of temporary democracy and anarchy, he prophesies that Europe will be eventually organized into a grand commonweal. Although in his

[39] *Ibid.*, II, 343-345.
[40] *Ibid.*, II, 346.
[41] *Ibid.*
[42] *Ibid.*, II, 370.

application of historical periodicity to the seven earlier centuries he has not progressed beyond his 1830 *aperçu,* his attitude toward democracy and his prophecy of a new positive organisation of society suggest the Saint-Simonians.

The second essay—" Early German Literature," finished by March 2, 1831—is more suggestive of alteration of the old material under Saint-Simonian influence than the first one is. In " Early German Literature " Carlyle again insists upon the alternation of poetic and didactic epochs. That is, after the heyday of chivalry and minstrelsy in the Twelfth Century, came the wane of chivalry and troubadour songs in the late Thirteenth. Life with its appurtenances disclosed more contradictions the more it was investigated. The Church no longer rose like a dome over a united folk, but appeared a narrow prison, full of uncleanness. All the better spirits had to murmur and struggle against its thraldom. Disputatious Schoolmen were questioning nature for an answer to its sphinx-riddle, so that man might morally live and not be devoured. In the physical sciences, Roger Bacon and Albert the Great were fearlessly extorting her secret.[43] Thus everywhere we see, says Carlyle, the image of contest and effort. The spirit of man, which was once in peaceful loving communion with the universe, now feels itself hampered and hemmed-in; it struggles valiantly for room. Power is the need, and knowledge is power. Thus intellect becomes the grand faculty, almost absorbing the other faculties. Poetry, the harmonious unison of man and nature, cannot flourish. The epoch becomes a didactic one.[44] The didactic epoch produced apologues, fables, and satires—verse, but not poetical verse.[45] Didacticism reached its acme in the Reformation, when it attained

[43] *Ibid.,* II, 280.   [44] *Ibid.,* II, 281.   [45] *Ibid.,* II, 283.

to poetic concentration. After Luther, the didactic tendency sank to a lower level.[46] We cannot say exactly
where either limit of the didactic era lies. At its beginning, it and the Minnesinger epoch overlap and
mingle for a century.[47] Not until almost our own era
has Inquiry partly reconciled itself to Belief.[48] Doubtless the time is coming when the poetical as well as the
logical faculties will be cultivated. Then fancy, humor,
and imagination, wherein lie the main elements of
spiritual life, will flourish in new vigor, in a new and
finer harmony with an improved understanding.[49] To
search out the causes of the great revolution, from the
early poetic era to the succeeding didactic era, would
lead us beyond our depth. But let us remark, says Carlyle, that the change is nowise a relapse or a fall from a
higher state of culture.[50] Rather it is a natural progress
and a higher development of culture. The progressive
stages of culture of the European mind and in European
literature are somewhat analogous to the growth-stages
in an individual's culture. At first comes the lyrical
gladness over the first revelation of a wonderful and
good universe. All is loved, and believed, and used; all
action is spontaneous. Then, later, the lyrical gladness
gives way to a collected thoughtfulness and energy. In
this stage of the long struggle toward manhood, contradictions are often met.[51] The heroic crusades and
tuneful chivalry were doings of the world's youth; to
which its manhood succeeded. Poetic recognition is
followed by scientific examination:

. . . the reign of Fancy . . . has ended; and now [i. e., during
the didactic era of the Fifteenth Century] Understanding
which when reunited to Poetry, will one day become Rea-

---

[46] *Ibid.*, II, 284.
[47] *Ibid.*, II, 285.
[48] *Ibid.*, II, 284.

[49] *Ibid.*, II, 332.
[50] *Ibid.*, II, 281-282.
[51] *Ibid.*, II, 282-283.

son and a nobler Poetry, has to do its part. Meantime, while there is no such union, but a more and more widening controversy, prosaic discord and the unmusical sounds of labour and effort are alone audible.[52]

Thus, in " Early German Literature," Carlyle discussed the periodic alternations of poetic and didactic epochs; pressed an analogy to the stages of an individual's culture; and insisted upon the old psychological distinction between Reason and Understanding, which he had got from Kant largely through Coleridge. On his earlier division of six centuries into two periods, he made no advance. But in his distinction between poetic and didactic epochs, he perhaps came a little closer than before to the Saint-Simonian distinction between organic and critical epochs. However, as has been explained, we cannot definitely assign any of the evidence exclusively to 1830 or exclusively to 1831.

While working at the essays just examined, Carlyle continued his series of comments to the effect that society was rotten, and that it would—and should—go to pieces. Doubtless the actual social and political milieu had much to do with the comments. But it is also significant that his comments are in line with the Saint-Simonian view, and are, in the last one of the series, to be pointed out in the next paragraph, specifically connected with the Saint-Simonian concept of historical periodicity. The first of these comments in the new year came the day that he finished the essay on Taylor's *Historic Survey*. The comment occurs in a letter to Napier,[53] then editor of *The Edinburgh Review*. Carlyle was suggesting that an essay on Jeremy Bentham would be preferable to an earlier-proposed essay on fashionable novels. An essay on Bentham, Carlyle said, should delineate Bentham's

[52] *Ibid.*, II, 283.   [53] Dated January 20, 1831.

place and working in this section of the world's history. Bentham will not be put down by logic, and should not be put down, for we need him greatly as a backwoodsman. . . . Bentham is a denyer: he denies with a loud and universally convincing voice: his fault is that he can *affirm* nothing, except that money is pleasant in the purse, and food in the stomach, and that by this simplest of all beliefs he can reorganise Society. He can shatter it in pieces—no thanks to him, for its old fastenings are quite rotten—but he cannot reorganise it; this is a work for quite others than he.[54]

And in his notebook on February 7th he made much the same observation on the condition of social institutions.

All Europe is in a state of disturbance, of Revolution. About this very time they may be debating the question of British 'Reform,' in London. . . . The times are big with change. Will *one* century of constant fluctuation serve us, or shall we need two? Their Parl. Reforms, and all that, are of small moment; a beginning (of good & evil) nothing more. The whole frame [55] of Society is rotten and must go for fuel-wood, and *where* is the new frame to come from? I know not, and no man knows.[56]

Again, a letter to John Carlyle, March 27th, shows Carlyle's attitude on the necessity and the desirability of complete change in the old social institutions. The whole world, he said, is " quitting its old anchorage and venturing into new untried seas with little science of sailing abroad. . . . " Then, after saying that neither he nor his brother is primarily interested in politics, he adds: " I know not whether, had I the power by speak-

[54] *Selection from the Correspondence of . . . Macvey Napier,* pp. 102-103. Incidentally it may be noted that Carlyle's attitude here toward liberals and radicals was in perfect harmony with the Saint-Simonian attitude toward them.

[55] The word used by the Saint-Simonians was *cadre.*

[56] *Two Note Books,* pp. 183-184. This notebook entry stands immediately after the one already referred to, in which Carlyle proposes to himself the writing of an essay on the Saint-Simonians.

ing a word to delay that consummation [social change]
or hasten it, I would speak the word." [57]

And finally, in the letter of May 17th to d'Eichthal,
Carlyle not only added to his series of remarks on the
rottenness or non-existence of society, but specifically
connected that notion with the Saint-Simonian doctrine. The bearings of that remark and its connection
with the Saint-Simonian concept of historical periodicity
can best be seen by considering the whole contents of
the letter. According to this May letter, Carlyle had
read attentively the various publications that had been
sent him in the second packet from Paris. His respect
for the members of the Society increased the more he
studied their productions. And he signified his desire
for still more information.[58] Though increasingly confused by their religious tendencies, he was so much
attracted to the Society that he urged the apostle to
visit him in Scotland. Another point is Carlyle's attitude toward democracy. After commenting upon the
political fermentation in Britain, he said that democracy had risen and would not stop until it had achieved
its rights. And he added that democracy was a poor
blind monster to believe that liberty resided in the electoral franchise and to believe it could gain freedom by
weaving its chains into festoons.[59] But, for us now, the

---

[57] Froude, *Thomas Carlyle* . . . *1795-1835*, II, 118.

[58] Another packet, he thought, was even then on the road (see *The
New Quarterly*, II, 284). Apparently it contained a collection of *Le
Globe* (see *Revue historique*, LXXXII, 297).

[59] The phrase *knitting its chains into festoons*, which appears also in
Sartor Resartus (p. 250) and in Carlyle's essay " Goethe's Works "
(*Essays*, II, 441), Carlyle himself in the latter work assigns to Goethe's
Venetian Epigrams.

After I had searched in vain for the phrase, Professor R. S. Collins
pointed it out to me in Goethe's 128-line poem entitled " Weissagungen
des Bakis," stanza 13 (*Goethes Sämmtliche Werke* [ed. K. Goedeke,
Stuttgart. Cotta, n. d.], Bd. I, 211.)

most important point of this letter of May 17th is its statement on the doctrine of the Saint-Simonian Society.

In short, were the Saint-Simonian doctrine stated as a mere scientific doctrine, or held out as the *Prophecy of an ultimate Perfection* towards which Society must more and more approximate,—I could with few reservations subscribe to it. . . . [A few sentences earlier, Carlyle had said:] your speculative opinions, political, moral, philosophical, for most part carry their own evidence, and find hearty assent with me; often, indeed, I discern therein only a more decisive systematic exposition of what I had already gathered elsewhere.[60]

Then he listed four elements in the Saint-Simonian teachings of which he especially approved. We are now concerned with only two. The first was the Saint-Simonian delineation of " our actual No-society." [61] And the second was the delineation " of the critical and the organic alternation in man's history. . . . " [61]

That May letter throws remarkable light upon Carlyle's early contact with the Saint-Simonian Society. As we close this chapter, it is proper to stress particularly two of the points brought out in the letter and in the chapter. That is, after Carlyle had studied the Saint-Simonian doctrines, he made a series of statements to the effect that the old society had been disrupted—or was in process of disintegration—and he let that series of statements culminate in express approval of the Saint-Simonian delineation of the disrupted condition of present society. And the next phrase of the letter, after that approval, conveyed his specific approval of the Saint-Simonian delineation of the alternation of organic and critical eras in history. The chapter summary that follows will set in proper

[60] *The New Quarterly*, II, 285.   [61] *Ibid.*

perspective those two points and various other points concerning the early months—almost a year—of Carlyle's relations with the Saint-Simonians.

The first year of Carlyle's acquaintance with the Saint-Simonian documents was drawing to a close as *Sartor* was drawing towards completion. Direct contact with Saint-Simonian thought had begun under circumstances favorable for influence. After reading at least three important publications by the Society—*Le Producteur, Aux Artistes,* and a number of issues of *L'Organisateur*—he reported that he found little or nothing to dissent from, and that the opinions therein expressed were often such as he had cherished and had attempted to express in his own way. Though puzzled by the religious views of the Society, he asked for further information, thus inviting further correspondence. Notwithstanding Goethe's warning, he continued to study the documents, and began to think of writing an essay upon the Society. In the winter, he translated Saint-Simon's last work, *Nouveau Christianisme,* and wrote a brief Introduction for it. Unfortunately, both translation and Introduction have disappeared. And since the two essays that he completed in winter and spring of 1831, on the history of German literature, are in part a reworking of material that has also disappeared, we cannot draw any clear conclusions from the evidence in them. But a series of comments from winter and spring, to the effect that present society was dead or doomed, culminated in his May letter to d'Eichthal, in which he expressed special approval of the Saint-Simonian delineation of the actual no-society of his time. The same letter also expressed his disapproval of democracy. By this time he had read—in addition to *L'Industrie, Nouveau Christianisme,* and the three Society publications just mentioned—considerable other important materials setting forth the views of the Society. That is, he had recently read the first year's *Exposition,* a number of further issues of *L'Organisateur,* and one or more occasional proclamations from the Society. And he now said that the more he studied the writings of the Society, the more his respect for the members increased. In spite of his increasing objection to their religious views, he invited further communication and additional information. He even urged one of the apostles to visit him in Scotland. His comment to this apostle, d'Eichthal, on the Society's non-religious teachings is worth repeating, even though it has just been quoted:

your speculative opinions, political, moral, philosophical, for most part carry their own evidence, and find hearty assent with me; often, indeed I discern therein only a more decisive systematic exposition of what I had already gathered elsewhere.

And a final point—of great importance in this study— is Carlyle's express approval of the Saint-Simonian concept of historical periodicity, or, as he put it, the Saint-Simonian delineation " of the critical and the organic alternation in man's history." Apparently during the months in which *Sartor* was taking shape, Carlyle had at last found in the Saint-Simonian writings a decisive systematic exposition of the historic process,—an exposition that interpreted to his satisfaction his political milieu as well as the great sweep of historical change over which he had long been struggling.[62]

[62] Incidentally, we may observe in this experience a parallel to other experiences in Carlyle's intellectual history. More than once his long gropings were finally polarized by the discovery of his desideratum lucidly expressed, and by his adoption of the expression that he found. Perhaps the most familiar examples are his gropings in Wertherism, which were polarized by Goethe, and his gropings in Calvinism, which were polarized by Fichte.

CHAPTER IV

FROM *Sartor Resartus* TO THE BEGINNINGS OF *The French Revolution* (1831-1834)

A few general observations concerning the years 1831-1834 will help clarify the matters about to be presented in this chapter. One of the first things to notice is the fact that Carlyle's place of residence changed. Indeed, the limits of this chapter coincide almost perfectly with changes in setting. In August 1831, he began a visit that was to keep him in London for seven months; some three years later, he took up permanent residence in the capital. The earlier of the changes from the moors to the capital was important. Through it, Carlyle came into personal contact, for the first time, with one of the ablest minds of the new English generation, John Stuart Mill. He broadened his contact with various publishers and publishing men. He held discussions with the Saint-Simonian missionaries in person and became more clearly aware of the fantastic turns the Society was taking. Then too the times were changing. England was passing, under his eyes, into its reform era. And from *Sartor* on, Carlyle in his works attempted more and more to speak to his times about the times. After *Sartor*, came "Characteristics." Then, with the death of Goethe, came repeated attempts to interpret the great German as an artist of the old generation with a social message for the new generation. And as he wrote those interpretations of the old artist, Carlyle was himself groping his way toward a new artistic expression for what he had made his own concept of history. Step by step, with the aid of his concept of historical periodicity, he had come to see the French Revolution as a lesson for Europe and as a warning for England. And finally he undertook to express that interpretation in artistic form that every Child of the Covenant might joy to hear. Meanwhile the evidence concerning his regard for the Saint-Simonians and for their—and his—concept of historical periodicity shifted to some extent its bearings and its medium of expression. That is, the evidence shows less and less interest, on Carlyle's part, in the current activities of the Society. And that evidence is no longer found chiefly in his correspondence with d'Eichthal, but in his works written for publication and in his correspondence with his brother and with John Stuart Mill.

Sartor Resartus, the first major work written after Carlyle became acquainted with the Saint-Simonian publications,[1] shows various evidences of its author's connection with the Saint-Simonian thought. The specific references to the Saint-Simonians are more extensive than in any other of Carlyle's works written for publication. Teufelsdröckh quotes

without censure that strange aphorism of Saint-Simon's, concerning which and whom so much were to be said: *" L'âge d'or, qu'une aveugle tradition a placé jusqu'ici dans le passé, est devant nous. . . ."* [2]

And Heuschrecke reports thus the last days with that same Teufelsdröckh:

[1] See *Letters of Thomas Carlyle, 1826-1836,* pp. 174, 183, 220. Though written entirely at Craigenputtock in 1830 and 1831, it was, immediately upon completion, brought up to London with the aim of publishing it as a word in season.

[2] *Sartor Resartus,* p. 236. This expression concerning the Golden Age occurs frequently in the Saint-Simonian productions. It served as motto on the title-page of *Le Producteur.* And in *Le Producteur,* I, 440, Carrel assigns the expression to Saint-Simon.

... when the *Saint-Simonian Society* transmitted its Propositions hither ... our Sage sat mute; and at the end of the third evening said merely: "Here also are men who have discovered, not without amazement, that Man is still Man; of which high, long-forgotten Truth you already see them make a false application." Since then, ... there passed at least one Letter with its Answer between Messieurs Bazard-Enfantin and our Professor himself; of what tenor can now only be conjectured. On the fifth night following, he was seen for the last time!

Has this invaluable man, so obnoxious to most of the hostile Sects that convulse our Era, been spirited away by certain of their emissaries; or did he go forth voluntarily to their head-quarters to confer with them and confront them? [3]

But that quotation and those references are not our chief concern now.

The chief concern now is the reflection in *Sartor* of the Saint-Simonian concept of historical periodicity. Like the Saint-Simonian documents, *Sartor* states the law of progressive periodic mutation. Through perpetual metamorphoses to better forms, says Carlyle, society lives through all time. [4] Occasionally, it sinks and immolates itself so that if may soar the higher. [5] In characterizing the alternate epochs that constitute each period, Carlyle follows both Goethe and the Saint-Simonians. Eras of faith, he says, alternate with eras of denial. Ever must the vernal growth and summer luxuriance of all opinions, spiritual representations and creations, follow autumnal decay and winter dissolution and be followed by them. Men live in time; and only in the transitory time-symbol is ever-motionless Eternity made manifest. [6] To present the notion of transition between periods, Carlyle elaborates the phoenix

---

[3] *Sartor Resartus,* pp. 296-297.   [5] *Ibid.,* p. 248. See also p. 244.
[4] *Ibid.,* p. 236.   [6] *Ibid.,* p. 112.

doctrine. That is, in the transition between the eras of
faith, says Carlyle, destruction of the old system and
creation of the new proceed together. The organic fila-
ments of the new spin themselves in the ashes of the
old.[7] In tracing the alternate epochs in past history,
Carlyle goes back only 300 years, instead of the 2,300
years of the Saint-Simonians. Thus he omits the whole
of the classical period, as well as the organic epoch from
the Catholic-feudal period. But he is writing specifically of his own times. The present era, he says, is one
of unbelief.[8] For the last 300 years—especially for the
last seventy-five years—religion, which is the pericar-
dial tissue of society, has been attacked. Now it is rent
in shreds. Society is consumptive, and can be regarded
as defunct.[9] Now is the night of the world, and the
stars are as if blotted out for a season.[10] The world is
sold to unbelief, and the temples crumble down.[11] Voltaire in religion [12] and Napoleon in polity [13] were both
destructives, who must be thanked for useful work,—
for burning away and destroying falsities. The liberals,
economists, and utilitarians will ultimately carry their
point too and will destroy most existing institutions.
Unfortunately they cannot rebuild where they have
destroyed. But we cannot hinder the destruction. Instead, we must account it inevitable and proper.[14] Society is not dead; only the mortal carcass is shuffled off
to assume a nobler one.[15] Because of such beliefs, Teu-

[7] *Ibid.*, pp. 244, 248, 236.
[8] *Ibid.*, p. 112.
[9] *Ibid.*, p. 232.
[10] *Ibid.*, p. 294. Harrold's note points out Carlyle's indebtedness to
Richter's Preface to *Hesperus* for the passage on the " Night of the
World."
[11] *Ibid.*, p. 161.
[12] *Ibid.*, p. 194.
[13] *Ibid.*, pp. 178-179.
[14] *Ibid.*, pp. 233-235.
[15] *Ibid.*, p. 236.

felsdröckh is willing to see the destruction of the old
forms of society go on, gradually and with moderation,
so that a new and better society may be built.[16]   The
solution of the problem of evil in each new era comes
out in different terms.   Always the solution of the last
era has become obsolete and unserviceable for the new
era.[17]   Religion is already weaving herself new ves-
tures.[18]   And are not steam engines [of the Industrial
Revolution] rapidly overturning the old system of society and preparing by indirect but sure methods industrialism and government by the wisest?[19]   For the
last half-century independence has been touted as a
virtue.   Fools! exclaims Carlyle; were superiors worthy
to govern, and you to obey, reverence for them were
your only possible freedom.   All independence is rebellion.[20]   The phoenix death-birth of society may require
a long time—say 200 years more of convulsion and con-
flagration—before we find ourselves in a living society
not fighting, but working.[21]   The present philosophy of
clothes promises to reveal new-coming eras, the already
budding germs of a nobler era in universal history.[22]
And a Volume Two, *On the Palingenesia, or Newbirth
of Society*, will deal with the development of the social
institutions of the future.[23]

Thus in Carlyle's first major writing after he had
come in contact with the Saint-Simonians, he used
direct quotation from their works and made specific
references to their Society.   He stated the law of progressive periodic mutation.   He characterized the alternate epochs of faith and denial in a way that suggests

[16] *Ibid.*   [17] *Ibid.*, p. 189.   [18] *Ibid.*, p. 216.
[19] *Ibid.*, p. 118.   *Industrialism* was a term sometimes used for *social-
ism* in the early Nineteenth Century. See *Post*, p. 105, and note 104.
[20] *Ibid.*, p. 233.   [22] *Ibid.*, p. 80.
[21] *Ibid.*, p. 237.   [23] *Ibid.*, p. 217.

both Goethe and the Saint-Simonians. And he stated
clearly the Saint-Simonian notion of transition between
periods. Ignoring classicism and the organic medieval
epoch, he dealt with only the most recent epoch of
denial. That is, he insisted upon the virtual non-existence of the old society; regarded the work of the liberal
destructives as necessary and proper and desirable, but
short of the high mark of reconstruction; and condemned independence and freedom under the same ban
with liberalism. In his comment on the future, he
looked forward to a *palingenesia* [24] of nobler social insti-

---

[24] The word *palingenesia* in this connection is a striking one. And
probably Carlyle owed the word, as well as much of the idea it expresses,
to the Saint-Simonians. *Palingenesia* it not a new term. It was a term
in Stoical philosophy, and was used by Cicero. It occurred in the Greek
New Testament. And in the late Eighteenth and early Nineteenth Centuries, it was used by Bonnet, Richter, William Taylor of Norwich, Coleridge, and Ballanche, before Carlyle used it. However, so far as I know,
Carlyle did not adopt it until he found it in the writings of the Saint-
Simonians. Then in *Sartor,* his first major work after reading the Saint-
Simonians, he employed it with the emphasis, variations, and repetitions
that suggest a new and valued acquisition. Indeed, the word *palingenesia*
or *palingenesie* occurs six times in *Sartor* (pp. 217, 255, 268, 269, 270,
297) and twice more by early 1833 (*Essays,* III, 120, and Froude,
Thomas Carlyle . . . 1795-1835, II, 276).
   The idea of new-birth, or re-birth, of society occurs frequently in
Friedrich Schlegel's work on the philosophy of history. But the word
that Schlegel uses to express it is *Wiederherstellung* (*Philosophie der
Geschichte,* I, 193, 265; II, 27, 116 [twice], 143, 159, 162, 178, 228-229
[in *Friedrich von Schlegels sämmtliche Werke,* Wien, 1846, Bde. XIII
and XIV].)
   There are some other points in Schlegel's philosophy of history that
may have seemed good to Carlyle. For example, (1) Schlegel, unlike
Fichte, uses sociological method. That is, he believes man's external
development is subject to certain natural historical laws, and he insists
that his own philosophy of history is derived from facts. (2) He finds
considerable evidence that the march of humanity, instead of being
straightforward, lies in a circuitous course (*ibid.,* I, 191). And (3) he
believes that the history of the race, as well as of nations, can be divided
into three epochs: childhood, mature vigor, and old age (*ibid.,* II, 49).
But in the first two of those points Schlegel seems a less convincing source
than the Saint-Simonians for Carlyle's thought. And when Schlegel risks

tutions under a new era of government by the wisest. These points, though not the most complete evidence that we are to see of Saint-Simonian influence, are nevertheless unmistakable.

During the early part of Carlyle's 1831 visit to London, his letter and journal references to the Saint-Simonians are on the whole favorable. Within his first few days in the capital, he discussed the Society in a public eating-house [25] and at a Presbyterian minister's tea.[26] Shortly after, he read Southey's denunciatory article on the Saint-Simonians, and condemned its lack of insight.[27] And at the beginning of October he wrote his third letter to d'Eichthal. The primary purpose of this letter seems to have been to introduce, to d'Eichthal and to the Society, Dr. John Carlyle, who was on his way to Italy. Carlyle stated his own wish, as well as his brother's wish, that John should familiarize himself as much as possible with the actual aspects of the Doctrine of Saint-Simon. And Carlyle, at least in October, wished to carry the relation with d'Eichthal still further. After stating his own plan to remain in London throughout the winter, he assured d'Eichthal that, if the promised apostolic mission to London should take place within the next three months, he would count upon having the earliest notice of d'Eichthal's arrival and would expect to see him often. Carlyle mentioned

such terms as " das *Wort,* die *Kraft* und das *Licht* " to represent " das dreifache göttliche Princip und der innere Eintheilungsgrund einer solchen Philosophie der Geschichte " (*ibid.,* I, 197), one feels that there was a greater community of thought between Schlegel and Coleridge than between Schlegel and Carlyle.

[25] *Two Note Books,* p. 193 (August 9th).
[26] *Ibid.,* p. 198 (August 15th).
[27] Froude, *Thomas Carlyle . . . 1795-1835,* II, 162. Southey's essay, purporting to be a review of *Doctrine de Saint-Simon. Exposition. Première Année,* was Article IV in *The Quarterly Review,* XLV (No. 90, July, 1831), pp. 407-450.

pleasant anticipations of leisurely discussions on the great matters with which the apostle was busy, and again assured him of a warm personal welcome. Two other points in this October letter demand attention here. One point concerns the translation of the *Nouveau Christianisme,* which Carlyle had failed to dispose of. He had intended, he said, to send a copy of it to d'Eichthal. But since the manuscript was at present in the hands of Dr. Bowring [28] and was therefore not available, he would have to await another opportunity. However, Carlyle stated his purpose eventually to put the translation at d'Eichthal's disposal. The final point for consideration concerning this October letter is Carlyle's expression of pleasure in regularly receiving the issues of the Saint-Simonian daily paper, *Le Globe.* In *Le Globe,* he said, he found information on various matters of much interest to him—matters that were understood only imperfectly, or not at all, in London.[29]

But some confusion—and disappointment too, on Carlyle's part—seems to have occurred near the time of the proposed apostolic mission to London. On October 10th Carlyle was elated at the prospect of seeing " Gustave d'Eichthal the St. Simonian this night! " [30] However, he was mistaken, as the next day's journal entry records. " Last night, saw Mill and d'Eichthal (Brother of Gustave the St. Simonian), and discoursed largely upon men and things." [31] Something in that discussion, or more likely, something in the internal developments and in the resulting dissensions of this

[28] John Bowring, editor of *The Westminster Review.*
[29] *The New Quarterly,* II, 288. Eugène d'Eichthal found a record that his father sent Carlyle a collection of *Le Globe* (see *Revue historique,* LXXXII, 297).
[30] *Two Note Books,* p. 201.
[31] *Ibid.,* p. 205.

time within the Society,[32] coupled with John Carlyle's written report on his observations in Paris, seems to have altered Carlyle's attitude toward the group. And near the middle of November, he wrote John, now in Florence,

I was much instructed by your sketches of Saint-Simonism; concerning which I do not differ far from you in opinion or prediction. It is an upholstery aggregation, not a Promethean creation; therefore cannot live long: yet the very attempt to rebuild the old dilapidated Temple, were it only with deals and canvas, is significant. . . . " [33]

Notwithstanding Carlyle's condemnation, late in 1831, of the current activities of the Society, his thought had taken on the dye of the Saint-Simonian concept of historical periodicity. One more illustration of that fact, before we turn to the " Characteristics," is found in a short notebook entry between November 2nd and 4th.

A common persuasion among serious ill-informed persons that the *end of the world* is at hand. . . . —So was it at the beginning of the Christian era; say rather, at the *termination* of the Pagan one.[34]

Brief as the entry is, it is shot through with suggestion of such elements as the Saint-Simonian designation of periods and epochs in past European history and the Saint-Simonian interpretation of alternate growth and

---

[32] In November 1831, occurred the split of the Saint-Simonians on the moral theories of Enfantin. The rupture extended even to the two Fathers of the Society, Bazard and Enfantin (see *Oeuvres de Saint-Simon et d'Enfantin* [Paris, 1865], IV, 154 ff.). Booth (*Saint-Simon and Saint-Simonism*, p. 133) comments that, in 1831, on the maxim that flesh is equal in dignity and sanctity to mind, rehabilitation of the flesh became a grand object of the Saint-Simonians. And, says Booth, in February 1832, even Olinde Rodrigues, the oldest disciple of Saint-Simon, withdrew from Enfantin because of Enfantin's views of women.

[33] *Letters of Thomas Carlyle, 1826-1836*, p. 267.

[34] *Two Note Books*, p. 223.

decay. Carlyle's correction of himself in the last clause
suggests something of the manner in which the Saint-
Simonian concept of periodicity had worked in his
thought.

Although " Characteristics," Carlyle's last production in 1831, contains no specific reference to the Saint-
Simonians, one passage in the essay is obviously
directed at them.

> . . . everywhere the eternal fact begins again to be recog-
> nised, that there is a Godlike in human affairs. . . . Such
> recognition we discern on all hands and in all countries: in
> each country after its own fashion. In France, among the
> younger nobler minds, strangely enough; where, in their
> loud contention with the Actual and Conscious, the Ideal
> and Unconscious is, for the time, without exponent; where
> Religion means not the parent of Polity, as of all that is
> highest, but Polity itself; and this and the other earnest
> man has not been wanting, who could audibly whisper to
> himself: " Go to, I will make a Religion." . . . Meanwhile
> let us rejoice rather that so much has been seen into, were
> it through never so diffracting media, and never so madly
> distorted; that in all dialects, though but half-articulately,
> this high Gospel begins to be preached: Man is still Man.[35]

Whatever condemnation of the Saint-Simonians there
is in this passage is condemnation of the religious short-
comings of the Society. Carlyle had all along ques-
tioned their religious views. Until lately at least, other
elements in their thought had met with his approval.

In " Characteristics " one detects traces—even if he
cannot prove all of them—of Saint-Simonian elements
fused with some of Carlyle's old philosophic doctrines.
For example, Carlyle's early suspicions of rationalism
may have fused with the Saint-Simonian notion of the
questioning attitude manifested during critical epochs
in society. But Carlyle goes much further than the

[35] *Essays*, III, 42.

Saint-Simonians, and actually denounces metaphysical speculation as a disease.[36] Thinking along that same line, he elaborates his doctrine of the Unconscious,[37] which is strongly reminiscent of the doctrine of the Dynamic earlier elaborated in " Signs of the Times." Furthermore, he clarifies his old " Signs of the Times " notion that the Idea rules the Actual. That is, he no longer oscillates between an *idea* in its psychological sense, and an *ideal*, or *principle*, in a sociological sense of the word. " Characteristics " says clearly that every society, every polity, has a spiritual principle, is an embodiment, tentative and more or less complete, of an Idea. And this Idea is ever a true loyalty.[38] Carlyle perhaps could have said, with about the same meaning, what he had found in Goethe and the Saint-Simonians: The Idea is ever a credible Belief, or interpretative schema. However, as before suggested, the infiltration of Saint-Simonian elements in these old lines of thought may not be clearly demonstrable.

But there can be no doubt of Saint-Simonian influence when we examine the concept of history in " Characteristics." For the sake of clarity and continuity in examining the numerous details of evidence, one should keep in mind the five main elements with which our analysis deals: the law of progress through periods, the palingenetic method of transition between periods, the characterization of the two kinds of epochs in each period, the application of the theory in the whole sweep of past European history, and the interpretation of the present and the future in the light of the periodic process.

As in *Sartor,* Carlyle here, in " Characteristics," again states the law of progressive periodic mutation and

[36] *Ibid.,* III, 25.   [37] *Ibid.,* III, 13.   [38] *Ibid.,* III, 14.

stresses transition between periods. All human things, he says, are by nature subject to movement and change, and man is regularly progressing.[39] That progress is periodic, rather than straightforward. Human society, like an individual, has times of vigor and times of sickness,—epochs of growth and epochs of decay. Every dissolution of society is followed by a new birth.[40]

What Carlyle calls the vigorous ages of society have the same characteristics as the Saint-Simonians' organic epochs of society. That is, both Carlyle and the Saint-Simonians insist that these ages, or epochs, are organized around credible principles, or schemata, that interpret all phenomena. Every society, says Carlyle, every polity, has a spiritual principle; is the embodiment, tentative and more or less complete, of an Idea. All its tendencies of endeavor, specialties of custom, its laws, politics, and whole procedure are prescribed by an Idea and follow naturally from it. This Idea is ever a true loyalty, and has in it something of a religious, paramount, quite infinite character; it is properly the soul of the state, its life.[41]

. . . if the mystic significance of the State . . . dwells vitally in every heart, encircles every life as with a second higher life, how should it stand self-questioning? It must rush outward, and express itself by works. Besides, if perfect, it . . . cannot be reasoned of; except *musically*, or in the language of Poetry, cannot yet so much as be spoken of.[42]

If in the widely separated times of the Roman Republic and feudal monarchy, society had its difficulties, it also had its strength. In those times,

[39] *Ibid.*, III, 37.
[40] *Ibid.*, III, 13 and 39.
[41] *Ibid.*, III, 14. The terminology thus far—that each society is the tentative embodiment of an Idea—probably goes back ultimately to Fichte's *Über das Wesen des Gelehrten* (see *ante*, p. 12, note 5a).
[42] *Ibid.*

Society went along without complaint . . . . Society was what we can call a *whole* . . . . For all men . . . were animated by one great Idea; thus all efforts pointed one way, everywhere there was *wholeness*. Opinion and Action had not yet become disunited; but the former could still produce the latter, or attempt to produce it . . . . Thought and the voice of thought were also a unison; thus, instead of Speculation, we had Poetry; Literature, in its rude utterance, was as yet a heroic Song, perhaps too a devotional Anthem.

Religion was everywhere; Philosophy lay hid under it, peaceably included in it. . . . Only at a later era must Religion split itself into Philosophies; and thereby, the vital union of Thought being lost, disunion and mutual collision in all provinces of Speech and Action more and more prevail.[43]

Apparently narrowing his discussion to the medieval era, of Mother Church and Chivalry, he says:

Action, in those old days, was easy, was voluntary, for the divine worth of human things lay acknowledged; Speculation was wholesome, for it ranged itself as the handmaid of Action; what could not so range itself died out by its natural death, by neglect. Loyalty still hallowed obedience, and made rule noble; there was still something to be loyal to: the Godlike stood embodied under many a symbol in men's interests and business; the Finite shadowed forth the Infinite; Eternity looked through Time.[44]

It is by Faith that man removes mountains: while he had Faith, his limbs might be wearied with toiling, his back galled with bearing; but the heart within him was peaceable and resolved.[45]

Thus much will suffice for Carlyle's characterization and designation of what he called the vigorous ages of society and what the Saint-Simonians called the organic epochs. Both agreed that the peculiar characteristic of those epochs was belief in some fundamental schemata that interpreted the phenomena of life. And both agreed that the epoch of the Roman Republic and the epoch of feudal monarchy showed those characteristics.

In the discussion of the disunited epochs that alternate with those vigorous, or united, epochs, there is almost as much agreement between Carlyle and the Saint-Simonians. The leading characteristics of the disunited, or critical, epochs is, for both of them, the lack of credible schemata, or principles, of society. Carlyle says:

> Only at a later era [than the Roman Republic or than feudal monarchy] must Religion split itself into Philosophies; and thereby, the vital union of Thought being lost, disunion and mutual collision in all provinces of Speech and Action more and more prevail.[46]

And he continues:

> Thus, not to mention other instances, one of them much nearer hand,—so soon as Prophecy among the Hebrews had ceased, then did the reign of Argumentation begin; and the ancient Theocracy, in its Sadduceeisms and Phariseeisms, and vain jangling of sects and doctors, give token that the *soul* of it had fled, and that the *body* itself, by natural dissolution, ' with the old forces still at work, but working in reverse order,' was on the road to final disappearance.[47]

After the illustration of a disunited decadent era in Hebrew history—which he owed to Goethe's suggestion, rather than to the Saint-Simonians—Carlyle shifted his attention to recent examples. It is our misfortune, he says, that " this is the age of Metaphysics, in the proper, or skeptical Inquisitory sense." But that misfortune is necessary:

. . . the arena of free Activity has long been narrow-

[46] *Ibid.*, III, 15-16.
[47] *Ibid.*, III, 16. Concerning the expression that Carlyle here put into quotation marks, see *Sartor*, p. 72.

ing, that of skeptical Inquiry becoming more and more universal, more and more perplexing. The Thought conducts not to the Deed; but in boundless chaos, self-devouring, engenders monstrosities, phantasms, fire-breathing chimeras.[48]

. . . the truth is, with Intellect, as with most other things, we are now passing from that first or boastful stage of Self-sentience into the second or painful one: out of these often-asseverated declarations that ' our system is in high order,' we come now, by natural sequence, to the melancholy conviction that it is altogether the reverse. . . . Never . . . was there, that we hear or read of, so intensely self-conscious a Society. Our whole relations to the Universe and to our fellow-man have become an Inquiry, a Doubt . . . .[49]

Belief, Faith has well-nigh vanished from the world. The youth on awakening in this wondrous Universe no longer finds a competent theory of its wonders. . . . the ancient ' ground-plan of the All ' belies itself when brought into contact with reality . . . . For young Valour and thirst of Action no ideal Chivalry invites to heroism, prescribes what is heroic: the old ideal of Manhood has grown obsolete, and the new is still invisible to us . . . .[50]

To the better order of such minds any mad joy of Denial has long since ceased: the problem is not now to deny, but to ascertain and perform. Once in destroying the False, there was a certain inspiration; but now the genius of Destruction has done its work, there is now nothing more to destroy. The doom of the Old has long been pronounced, and irrevocable; the Old has passed away: but, alas, the New appears not in its stead; the Time is still in pangs of travail with the New.[51]

Those characterizations and designations of disunited epochs in history, with the great stress on the most recent one and its lack of a unifying schema, furnish an excellent example of the fusion of the elements from Goethe with the more elaborate and inclusive concept of the Saint-Simonians.

[48] *Essays*, III, 27.   [50] *Ibid.*, III, 29.
[49] *Ibid.*, III, 19.   [51] *Ibid.*, III, 32.

Then he brings his long parergon up against his text—the two books that "Characteristics" purports to review.[52]   And turning his attention to the point at which the present merges over into the future, Carlyle counsels hope.   Notable attempts, he believes, are already being made to formulate the new constructive, or organizing, schema that will serve to unite the coming era.

> . . . both these Philosophies [Schlegel's and Hope's] are of the Dogmatic or Constructive sort: . . . an endeavour to bring the Phenomena of man's Universe once more under some theoretic Scheme . . . .[53]

Indeed one of the signs of the times is the growing tendency of thinkers to deal in affirmation rather than in mere denial.

> . . . Faith in Religion has again become possible and inevitable for the scientific mind . . . .   Nay, in the higher Literature of Germany, there already lies . . . the beginning of a new revelation of the Godlike . . . .[54]

And everywhere—in England and in France, as well as in Germany—the eternal fact begins again to be recognized, that there is a Godlike in human affairs.[55]   True, the essay "Signs of the Times," written in 1829, had closed with a similar note of hope.   But it is worth observing that the hope in "Characteristics," late 1831, is based upon, and culminates in, a philosophy of history far more elaborate and sociologically satisfying than the earlier general faith in progress and the psychologically based notion of alternation between dynamics and mechanics.

[52] Friedrich von Schlegel's *Philosophische Vorlesungen, insbesondere über Philosophie der Sprache und des Wortes* (Vienna, 1830), and Thomas Hope's *An Essay on the Origin and Prospects of Man* (London, 1831).
[53] *Essays*, III, 33.   [54] *Ibid.*, III, 41.   [55] *Ibid.*, III, 42.

Thus much of the disunited past and present epochs in society—with a strong note of hope for a united and faithful future—we find in "Characteristics." Carlyle's notion of the characteristic disunity and lack of fundamental organizing schemata in such epochs exactly corresponds with the Saint-Simonian characterization of critical epochs. Although Carlyle introduced from Hebrew history an illustration that he had obviously elaborated from Goethe rather than from the Saint-Simonians, he does discuss in considerable detail, as do the Saint-Simonians, the contemporary era as an example.

Having analyzed Carlyle's concept of history in " Characteristics " with respect to periodic progress, palingenetic transition between periods, alternating epochs of organization and lack of organization around fundamental schemata, his designation of various epochs of both sorts in the past, and his note of hope about an inevitable epoch of affirmation and faith in the future, we are ready to follow some further sweeping comments on change and the nature of change in society. These comments bear especially on the notion of palingenetic transition. But they also clarify and synthesize the other details of the whole process that we have analyzed in the essay.

For ourselves, the loud discord which jars . . . in all the Thought and Action of this period [i. e., epoch, or era], does not any longer utterly confuse us.[56] . . . The progress of man towards higher and nobler developments . . . lies not only prophesied by Faith, but now written to the eye of Observation . . . .[57] . . . In all ages, . . . questions of Death and Immortality, Origin of Evil, Freedom and Necessity, must, under new forms, anew make their appearance; ever, from time to time, must the attempt to shape for ourselves some Theorem of the Universe be repeated.[58]

---

[56] *Ibid.*, III, 36.   [57] *Ibid.*, III, 37.   [58] *Ibid.*, III, 25.

For that reason, says Carlyle, the disease of metaphysics is a perennial one.[59]   But

. . . there is a better and worse in it; a stage of convalescence, and a stage of relapse with new sickness: these forever succeed each other, as is the nature of all Lifemovement here below.   The first, or convalescent stage, we might . . . name that of Dogmatical or Constructive Metaphysics; when the mind constructively endeavours to scheme out and assert for itself an actual Theorem of the Universe, and therewith for a time rests satisfied.[60]

All theologies and sacred cosmogonies belong to that dogmatical, or constructive, stage of metaphysics.[61]

The second or sick stage might be called that of Skeptical or Inquisitory Metaphysics; when the mind having widened its sphere of vision, the existing Theorem of the Universe no longer answers the phenomena, no longer yields contentment; but must be torn in pieces, and certainty anew sought for in the endless realms of denial.[62]

All Pyrrhonisms belong to this skeptical stage, which is a pure, but a necessary, evil.[63]

How often, in former ages, by eternal Creeds, eternal Forms of Government and the like, has it been attempted, fiercely enough, and with destructive violence, to chain the Future under the Past; and say to . . . Providence . . . : Hitherto shalt thou come, but no farther! A wholly insane attempt; and for man himself, could it prosper, . . . a very Life-in-Death. . . . could you ever establish a Theory of the Universe that were entire, unimprovable, and which needed only to be got by heart; man then were spiritually defunct . . . .   But the gods . . . have forbidden such suicidal acts. As Phlogiston is displaced by Oxygen, and the Epicycles of Ptolemy by the Ellipses of Kepler; so does Paganism give place to Catholicism, Tyranny to Monarchy,

[59] *Ibid.*
[60] *Ibid.*, III, 26.
[61] *Ibid.*
[62] *Ibid.*
[63] *Ibid.*, III, 26-27.

and Feudalism to Representative Government,—where
also the process does not stop.[64]

. . . In change . . . is nothing terrible . . . : on the contrary, it lies in the very essence of our lot and life in this
world.. . . . Change, indeed, is painful; yet ever need-
ful . . . . Nay, if we look well to it, what is all Derange-
ment, and necessity of great Change, in itself such an evil,
but the product simply of *increased resources* which the old
methods can no longer administer; of new wealth which the
old coffers will no longer contain? What is it, for example,
that in our own day bursts asunder the bonds of ancient
Political Systems, and perplexes all Europe with the fear of
Change, but even this: the increase of social resources,
which the old social methods will no longer sufficiently
administer? [65]

In economics, it is true again: the old methods of
administration will no longer suffice.[66] So too in metaphysics, which, if a necessary evil, is the forerunner of
much good. What is skepticism but the sour fruit of a
most blessed increase: increase of knowledge? If skepticism produces no affirmation, it destroys much negation. And faith again becomes possible and inevitable.[67]
Thus for Carlyle in " Characteristics " the hope of the
future and the realization of the past, with all their
alternations of affirmation and denial, were linked together in a progressive philosophy of history, arrived at
by a sociological method rather than a metaphysical
one.

In " Characteristics," as has been shown, Carlyle
gives his clearest and his fullest statement, thus far, of
his philosophy of historical periodicity. Human progress proceeds, he says, through alternate epochs of affirmative, or constructive, unity and skeptical disunity.
In the vitally unified epochs, thought and activity are

[64] *Ibid*, III, 37-38.
[65] *Ibid.*, III, 39.
[66] *Ibid.*
[67] *Ibid.*, III, 40-41.

organized around credible schemata, or principles, that
interpret all the phenomena and serve their times adequately as ground-plans, or theoria, of the universe.
Those epochs are epochs of religion and faith. But at
best those schemata, ground-plans, or theoria of the
universe are, and must be, only temporary approximations to the truth. Eventually mind widens its sphere
of vision; and the existing theorem of the universe no
longer answers the phenomena, no longer yields contentment. The old coffers will no longer contain the
new wealth; the old methods can no longer administer
the new increase of resources. The old organization and
theorem must be torn to pieces, and certainty anew
sought for in the realms of denial. The vital union of
thought being lost, disunion and mutual collision in all
provinces of thought and action more and more prevail.
Such epochs are epochs of skepticism, when man's whole
relation to the universe and to his fellowman becomes
an inquiry, a doubt. But along with the disruption of
the old forms of the organizing principle comes reincar-
nation into fairer forms. With the decadence of the
old society comes newbirth. Thus by late 1831, Carlyle's theory of historical periodicity includes Goethe's
theory and has become more elaborate than it. But it
corresponds to the Saint-Simonian theory in general and
in a number of details. Furthermore, in Carlyle's tracing of the theory, or concept, in actual history, there is
considerable, but not so complete, correspondence with
the Saint-Simonians. Of what he calls the vitally united
epochs—the organic epochs of the Saint-Simonians—in
past history, " Characteristics " comments on three: the
age of the Hebrew prophets, the age of Roman paganism
and republicanism, and the age of Catholicism and
feudal monarchy. Obviously Carlyle's comment on the
first of those ages owes its presence here to Goethe

rather than to the Saint-Simonians. On the two other vital ages of the past, Carlyle offers little discussion. And he makes only slight characterization of what he hopes will be a fourth vital epoch, in the future. Of what he calls the skeptically disunited epochs—the critical epochs of the Saint-Simonians—he mentions only two: the post-prophetic age among the Hebrews and the present age without faith. The first of these again derives from Goethe. But the other epoch—the present, which is the theme of " Characteristics "—is discussed in much detail. That discussion shows great reliance upon the Saint-Simonian analysis. Indeed, Carlyle had unfolded the whole strongly derivative philosophy of history as it occurs in this essay as a back-drop against which to throw the present age in relief. If in this unfolding of his mature philosophy of history, the process of change and the manifold phenomena of discord that he found around him no longer utterly confused him, he owed his equanimity in very considerable part to the Saint-Simonians. The gift is largely theirs. They had stimulated and confirmed his own insights into history and had guided him in elaborating Goethe's general concept. They had helped him catch a ground-plan of the all, the scheme of change, which he had measured against his prophet and against actual history, and found good. And he believed it worth repeating. This philosophy of historical periodicity was to serve him well in the years ahead.

Carlyle's direct personal association with the apostles of the Saint-Simonian Society did not begin until early 1832. And it was brief. Although the recent fantastic developments and consequent dissentions among the Saint-Simonians may not have prejudiced Carlyle's opinion of the two missionaries personally, Enfantin's notions of rehabilitating the flesh seem to have been in Carlyle's mind when he met Gustave d'Eichthal. The meeting took place on the night of January 21, 1832, when Carlyle returned to his lodging after a dinner with James Fraser. He found d'Eichthal waiting for him. At the first interview he recognized that Gustave, at least, was " cleanly pure ":

A little, tight, cleanly pure lovable *Geschöpfchen*: a pure martyr and apostle, as it seems to me; almost the only one (not 'belonging to the Past') whom I have met with in my pilgrimage. . . . . His ideas narrow, and sore distorted; but his mind open, his heart noble.[68]

This estimate in several particulars anticipates Carlyle's estimate of Emerson many months later. Jane Carlyle too commented on the meeting with the Frenchman in 1832. After characterizing d'Eichthal in some of the same words that Carlyle had used, she pronounced his companion, Duveyrier, perhaps the stronger and the nobler of the two.[69] Carlyle, she added, was especially taken with d'Eichthal. But Carlyle's own comment to Macvey Napier two weeks later is off-hand and patronizing in tone: " We have two Saint-Simonian Missionaries here; full of earnest zeal; copious enough in half-true, and to me rather wearisome jargon." [70]

He was apparently giving the missionaries to understand somewhat the same estimate that he had written Napier of them. At all events, on February 15th, he wrote d'Eichthal—instead of seeing him, wrote him—

[68] *Two Note Books*, p. 248.

[69] Froude, *Thomas Carlyle . . . 1795-1835*, II, 181-182. Froude's date of December 1831 must be wrong. Possibly Jane did begin the letter to the Carlyle family in Scotland during December. But the meeting here reported took place after Carlyle had dined with Fraser (see *ibid.*, II, 182). That dining took place on January 21st (*ibid.*, II, 218, and *Two Note Books*, pp. 248-252).

[70] *Selection from the Correspondence of . . . Macvey Napier*, p. 123 (February 6, 1832).

the letter that proved to be the last one of their correspondence. This final letter of the correspondence deals chiefly with Carlyle's translation of the *Nouveau Christianisme*. Early in October, he had generously promised to turn over the unpublished translation to d'Eichthal.[71] But at that time Bowring, the editor of *The Westminister Review,* had it. Still later, it had been passed on to some " Magazine " editor [72]—Maginn, of *Fraser's Magazine,* I believe. But still the translation remained unpublished.[73] To fulfill the promise and to conclude his connection with the matter, Carlyle now sent the work to d'Eichthal—sent the translation, accompanied by the Introductory Notice and an explanatory letter. One statement in the letter indicates, though only vaguely, the tenor of the Introductory Notice:

. . . j'y [i. e., in the Introductory Notice] exprime sincèrement mon impression sur l'influence possible de Saint-Simon et de son écrit sur notre public anglais, et cela dans des termes plutôt en dessous qu'au dessus de l'opinion que je me suis faite de ce dernier écrit [i. e., *Nouveau Christianisme*] (ce à quoi j'étais naturellement forcé).[74]

The letter assumed, as it were protectively, that this Translator's Notice would at present be useless to d'Eichthal. But the translation itself Carlyle put at

[71] *Revue historique,* LXXXII (1903), 301.

[72] *Ibid.,* LXXXII, 304-305.

[73] Some years ago, I suggested that the article " Letter on the Doctrine of St.-Simon," *Fraser's Magazine,* V (July 1832), 666-669, was a re-working—with or without Carlyle's approval—of Carlyle's Introductory Notice. For evidence, see *Notes and Queries,* CLXXI (1936), 290-293. I now believe that the manuscript of Carlyle's translation of the *Nouveau Christianisme* and his Introduction to that translation will ultimately be found among Enfantin's papers in Bibliotheque de l'Arsenal in Paris. However, two attempts (1938 and 1939) to direct searchers to it have proved unsuccessful.

[74] *Revue historique,* LXXXII, 304-305.

d'Eichthal's disposal. He added in italics his sole condition: that *my name be not mentioned*.[75] Already,
Carlyle's earlier active interest in the work was dead:
" Ma tâche, en ce qui concerne ce sujet, est, je le crois,
maintenant accomplie." [76]

Although as European thinkers the Saint-Simonians
were rapidly passing their zenith, they had already made
considerable impression on the minds of several Britons
besides Carlyle.[77] Perhaps the most notable was John
Mill. Indeed, one of the last issues of *Le Globe* carried
a full front-page article by him, in which he lauded the
Society.[78] He had long been deeply interested in the
thought, the activity, and the individual members of
the group. The evidence of chief importance to the
present study is found in his autobiography and his
letters. It shows that he was impressed by the Saint-
Simonian concept of historical periodicity. An important passage from the *Autobiography* runs as follows:

The writers by whom, more than by any others, a new
mode of political thinking was brought home to me, were

[75] " que *mon nom ne soit pas mentionné*." *Ibid.*, LXXXII, 304.

[76] *Ibid.*, LXXXII, 305. As Carlyle in 1866 looked back over these
months of his early life in London, he remembered the Saint-Simonians
as " stirring and conspicuous objects in that epoch . . . now fallen all
dark and silent again." Froude, *Thomas Carlyle . . . 1795-1835*, II,
181, note 2.

[77] On September 12, 1831, some Dr. C . . . of London (identity
unknown; probably not Dr. John Carlyle) wrote to the Saint-Simonians
in Paris a highly complimentary letter. Dr. C . . . believed the time
ripe for sending missionaries to England. He himself had already translated and read before a numerous public the first twelve séances of
Exposition of the First Year. Sending four of those translated séances
to the editor of *Le Globe*, he urged that they be published in English.
And he stated his belief that the Saint-Simonian journals would soon be
published in England. See pamphlet entitled *Religion Saint-Simonienne*
(Paris, 1831), pp. 30-31. (A copy of this pamphlet is in the possession
of Duke University Library).

[78] A short paper identifying Mill's article and re-printing it has been
accepted for publication in *The Journal of the History of Ideas*.

those of the St. Simonian school in France. . . . [Mill here indicates that he became acquainted with some of their writings in 1829, while they were still in the earlier stages of their speculations] . . . . I was greatly struck with the connected view which they for the first time presented to me, of the natural order of human progress; and especially with their division of all history into organic periods [i. e., epochs] and critical periods [i. e., epochs]. . . . [Mill here defines and sketches the various epochs]. . . . These ideas, I knew, were not peculiar to the St. Simonians; on the contrary, they were the general property of Europe, or at least of Germany and France, but they had never, to my knowledge, been so completely systematized as by these writers, nor the distinguishing characteristics of a critical period [i. e., epoch] so powerfully set forth; for I was not then acquainted with Fichte's Lectures on 'the Characteristics of the Present Age.' . . . [Mill then alludes to Carlyle's denunciations of the present age of unbelief]. . . . But all that was true in these [Carlyle's] denunciations, I thought that I found more calmly and philosophically stated by the St. Simonians.[79]

And in a letter to Gustave d'Eichthal on November 7, 1829, Mill makes somewhat the same favorable comment on the Saint-Simonian philosophy of history.

Sans le vouloir, je viens de développer longuement une des parties les plus intéressantes de la philosophie Saint-Simonienne, quoiqu'elle ne lui appartienne pas exclusivement, à savoir: la distinction entre la *partie critique* et la *partie organique* de toute philosophie, et entre les époques critiques et organiques de l'esprit humain.[80]

In examining those statements by Mill, we must recall that during Carlyle's visit to London, in 1831-1832,

[79] J. S. Mill, *Autobiography* (edited by J. J. Coss, New York, 1924), pp. 114-116.

[80] J. S. Mill, *Correspondance inéditée avec Gustave d'Eichthal* (ed. Eugène d'Eichthal, Paris, 1898), pp. 31-32. Other striking comments by Mill on the Saint-Simonians can be found in this volume of letters and in the two volumes edited by H. S. R. Elliot in 1910.

Mill was perhaps his most intimate associate. And when Carlyle returned to Scotland, and the Saint-Simonians, shortly before their trial, gave up their great publishing program and went into a kind of monastic seclusion, Mill became Carlyle's chief source of information about their doings and sufferings.

Mill was not the only one of Carlyle's associates impressed by the Saint-Simonians. Some writer, or combination of writers, for *Fraser's Magazine* was also strongly impressed in 1832. Oliver Yorke's section in the February issue of *Fraser's* is an imaginary dialogue between Yorke [81] and Goethe. It comments upon Carlyle as a literary critic, alludes to some connection between that critic and *Fraser's*, and discusses briefly Saint-Simon's contribution to European thought. Yorke's statement that Saint-Simon's views contained some truths, but also might contain some errors in the application of those truths, reminds us of Carlyle's own safe comment to the same effect. Yorke then adds that Saint-Simon in his idea of progress confessed obligations to German thought. And the Goethe of this imaginary conversation responds by attributing an important degree of originality to Saint-Simon's concept of historical periodicity. Saint-Simon, says this hypothetical Goethe,

discovered, however, that this progress had not gone on at an equal rate in all time and place; that it was more rapid in its advances on the first promulgation of Christianity than it has been since. He has, accordingly, divided the different stages of this progress into distinct epochs, organic and critical. In organic epochs men sail, as it were, down 'the mighty stream of Tendency,' as your great poet, Wordsworth, writes; while, in critical ones, men have lost the current, and social activity errs, without object, into indeterminate wanderings. Christianity delivered the world from the critical epoch into which it had advanced from

[81] Maginn?

the introduction of Greek philosophy. The organic epoch, thus begun, concluded with Luther, and another critical epoch ensued, to which St. Simon is about to put an end.[82]

So runs the product of ambrosial nights around the *Fraser's* editorial table. Carlyle's relations with *Fraser's Magazine*, if never satisfactory to him, were at least useful to him in 1832. And in early 1832, he was more firmly connected with the ambiguous *Fraser's* group than with any other editors in London.

In estimating Carlyle's relations with Saint-Simonian thought during this London visit, it is certainly worth remembering that the personal friend Mill, whom he valued most highly during those years, and the publishing group that collaborated on *Fraser's* and most frequently printed Carlyle's articles, were both impressed by the Saint-Simonians. Both friend and publisher-group, as we have seen, put stress upon the Saint-Simonian concept of historical periodicity. To the latter, the concept seemed to have the value of originality; to the former, it provided a new mode of political thinking. What Carlyle, in his own adherence to the Saint-Simonian concept of historical periodicity, owed to those two widely different reinforcements must of course remain a matter of conjecture. But at this stage of his acquaintance with Mill, Carlyle was less liable than in the next decade to undervalue the sharpness of Mill's philosophic insight and the extent of his historical and political knowledge. I feel that at least Mill's approval of the Saint-Simonian concept of historical periodicity

---

[82] " Oliver Yorke at Home. No. III. A Dialogue with Johann Wolfgang von Goethe," *Fraser's Magazine*, V (February, 1832), 32-33. Elsewhere (*Notes and Queries*, CLXXI [1936], 290-293) I have discussed the relation of the " Letter on the Doctrine of St.-Simon," which appeared in the July issue of *Fraser's* (pp. 666-669), to the translator's notice that Carlyle wrote in 1830 for his English version of *Nouveau Christianisme*.

had something to do with fixing it forever in Carlyle's philosophy of history.

During the rest of Carlyle's visit to London, he continued his prophecy of social destruction and palingenesia. That prophecy, as we have seen in *Sartor* and in " Characteristics," was carefully founded upon the notion that periodicity is a basic law of human history. The whole philosophy of course did not need to be explained in the letter of January 10th to John Carlyle, who knew his brother well. The letter alluded to the proof-reading of " Characteristics " and to the Whig editor Napier's comment that the essay was " inscrutable."

. . . my own fear [added Carlyle] was that it might be too *scrutable*; for it indicates decisively enough that Society (in my view) is utterly condemned to destruction, and even now beginning its travail-throes of Newbirth.[83]

Through the winter Carlyle worked at the twin essays on Biography and on Boswell's *Life of Johnson,* and finished them early in March. The latter essay, using the philosophy of history that Carlyle had fused out of the harmonious doctrines in Goethe and the Saint-Simonians, characterized the age of Johnson thus:

It was wholly a divided age, that of Johnson; Unity existed nowhere, in its Heaven, or in its Earth. Society, through every fibre, was rent asunder: all things, it was then becoming visible, but could not then be understood, were moving onwards, with an impulse received ages before, yet now first with a decisive rapidity, towards that great chaotic gulf, where, whether in the shape of French Revolutions, Reform Bills, or what shape soever, bloody or bloodless, the descent and engulfment assume, we now see them weltering and boiling. . . . HYPOCRISY and ATHEISM are already, in silence, parting the world. Opinion and Action . . . have commenced their open quarrel . . . .

[83] *Letters of Thomas Carlyle, 1826-1836,* p. 284.

. . . Denial waxed stronger and stronger, Belief sunk more and more into decay.[84]

If the last part of the quotation recalls the Goethe passage on *Glauben* and *Unglauben,* the first part recalls the Saint-Simonian characterization of the most recent critical epoch. Two harmonious elements had been joined, and they were not to be put asunder. Elsewhere in the essay Carlyle insists that Johnson had in him the stuff of kings—if he had only lived in an era that would have reverenced its kingly characters. " Had the golden age of those new French Prophets, when it shall be *à chacun selon sa capacité, à chaque capacité selon ses oeuvres,* but arrived! " [85]   The quotation is of course from the Saint-Simonians.[86]

Immediately upon his return to Scotland, Carlyle received news that Goethe was dead. Consequently, much of Carlyle's writing in the next six months reflects special interest in that patriarch of German literature. The Scot was attempting to state the great German's significance to the age. Although during this time Carlyle only once discussed the sadly embarrassed Saint-Simonians,[87] their philosophy of history, which had

[84] *Essays,* III, 104-105.

[85] *Ibid.,* III, 92.

[86] The quotation occurs frequently as a motto in the Saint-Simonian publications. For example, the 18th issue of the 7th year of *Le Globe* (January 18, 1831, p. 69), which was the first issue to carry the subtitle *Journal de la doctrine de Saint-Simon,* displays the quotation as one of the three mottoes on the front page. When on January 1, 1832 (issue 1 of the 8th year, p. 1), the subtitle again changed and became *Journal de la religion de Saint-Simonienne,* one of the five mottoes on the front page was " A chacun selon sa vocation. A chacun selon ses oeuvres." *L'Organisateur* (issue 1 of 2nd year, August 27, 1830, p. 1) bore as one of its three mottoes " A chacun selon sa capacité, à chaque capacité selon ses oeuvres." Much the same idea is expressed in Séance VII of the First Year's *Exposition* of the Doctrine de Saint-Simon (p. 255).

[87] *Letters of Thomas Carlyle to John Stuart Mill, John Sterling and Robert Browning* (ed. by A. Carlyle, London, Unwin, 1923), p. 9 (June

fused with Goethe's *Glauben-Unglauben* notion, may have lain behind several of his interpretations and comments. The essay " The Death of Goethe," which was finished by April 26th, says of Goethe:

The gulf into which this man ventured, which he tamed and rendered habitable, was the greatest and most perilous of all, wherein truly all others lie included: *The whole distracted Existence of man in an age of Unbelief.*[88]

And at the same time concerning Goethe's *Works,* he wrote:

Wondrously, the wrecks and pulverised rubbish of ancient things, institutions, religions, forgotten noblenesses, made alive again by the breath of Genius, lie here in new coherence and incipient union, the spirit of Art working creative through the mass; that *chaos,* into which the eighteenth century with its wild war of hypocrites and sceptics had reduced the Past, begins here to be once more a *world.* —This, the highest that can be said of written Books, is to be said of these: there is in them a New Time, the prophecy and beginning of a New Time. The corner-stone of a new social edifice for mankind is laid there . . . .[89]

The later essay entitled " Goethe's *Works,*" finished about July 13th, says much the same thing, in words a little more suggestive of the concept of historical periodicity:

Thus, from our point of view, does Goethe rise on us as the Uniter, the victorious Reconciler, of the distracted, clashing elements of the most distracted and divided age that the world has witnessed since the Introduction of the Christian Religion, to which old chaotic Era, of world-confusion and world-*re*fusion, of blackest darkness, succeeded by a

16, 1832). Again *ibid.,* p. 19 (October 16th), he mentions the Trial of the Saint-Simonians. In neither letter does he refer to their philosophy of history.

[88] *Essays,* II, 379.

[89] *Ibid.,* II, 381.

dawn of light and nobler 'dayspring from on high,' this wondrous Era of ours is, indeed, oftenest likened. To the faithful heart let no era be a desperate one! It is ever the nature of Darkness to be followed by a new nobler Light; nay, to produce such. . . . by natural vicissitude, the age of *Persiflage* goes out, and that of earnest unconquerable Endeavour must come in: for the ashes of the old fire will not warm men anew . . . .[90]

By August 12th, Carlyle had written his commentary on Goethe's *The Tale*. In it he adopted some of the editorial machinery used in *Sartor*, and put his most amazing comments into notes signed by the initials of Diogenes Teufelsdröckh. Concerning the four kings— Golden King, Silver King, Brazen King, and Mixed-metal King—Teufelsdröckh says:

Consider these Kings as Eras of the World's History; no, not as Eras, but as Principles which jointly or severally rule Eras. Alas, poor we, in this chaotic, soft-soldered 'transitory age,' are so unfortunate as to live under the Fourth King.[91]

. . . here is a wonderful EMBLEM OF UNIVERSAL HISTORY set forth; more especially a wonderful Emblem of this our wonderful and woful " Age of Transition " . . . .[92]

Finally, may I take leave to consider this *Mährchen* as the deepest Poem of its sort in existence, as the only true Prophecy emitted for who knows how many centuries?[93]

The first of Teufelsdröckh's eras, if we interpret it in the light of " Characteristics " and Goethe's " Israel in der Wüste," may possibly be the Hebrew era of prophecy. The other three eras may have some remote connection with the Pagan, the Catholic, and the new Industrial Hierarchy periods of the Saint-Simonians.

[90] *Ibid.*, II, 434.   [91] *Ibid.*, II, 459, note 3.   [92] *Ibid.*, II, 449.
[93] *Ibid.*, II, 479, note 2. Teufelsdröckh's allegory of the four kings may have some connection with Sauerteig's four methods of interpreting history in " Cagliostro," 1833.

But all that can be said with certainty is that Carlyle was struggling for an artistic representation of his philosophy of history. Perhaps that fact throws some light on the fantastic nature of Teufelsdröckh's footnotes of literary interpretation. True, Carlyle's interpretations of Goethe's significance earlier in the summer had been extravagant too. But in then proclaiming Goethe the victorious reconciler of the clashing elements of the Eighteenth Century, Carlyle was at least consistent with the philosophy of history that he had already presented in *Sartor* and " Characteristics."

In the summer and again in the fall of 1832, probably as a result of his preoccupation with Goethe, Carlyle made two excellent translations of the passage already quoted from Goethe's " Israel in der Wüste." He certainly had known the passage for a year, since he had echoed it in *Sartor*. Probably he had known it much longer. But the translation in his notebook, between July 22nd and August 8th,[94] seems to be his first direct quotation of this extremely important interpretation of history. As Professor Harrold has pointed out, the passage is important for Carlyle's notion of survival of the worthiest in history, as well as for the notion of historical periodicity.[94a] But at present we are interested in only the latter notion. True, Goethe's interpretation of history, which has already been quoted in this study,[95] does contain the notion of alternating epochs in

---

[94] Froude, *Thomas Carlyle . . . 1795-1835*, II, 230-231.

[94a] *Carlyle and German Thought: 1819-1834*, p. 176. It is perhaps worth pointing out that a statement of the survival of the worthy occurs in Carlyle's 1830 manuscript *History of German Literature*, p. 13: " Nothing that has not some degree of perennial intrinsic worth, by whatever name we may call it, will be permanently remembered." Perhaps the diction in that 1830 manuscript passage shows some resemblance to Goethe's diction. Two more passages in Carlyle's 1830 manuscript (pp. 14-15 and p. 20) deal with the idea of survival.

[95] *Vide supra*, p. 24.

human history, does characterize though briefly the
alternating epochs by the terms belief and unbelief, and
does—in the sentences immediately following the ones
Carlyle quoted—designate an epoch of belief and an
epoch of unbelief in Hebrew history. On the other
hand, the passage and its context fall far short of the
concept of historical periodicity that Carlyle had
already used. Many details concerning the respective
epochs, the whole *modus operandi* of the phoenix-like,
or palingenetic, transition between periods, and the
whole tracing-out of the periods in European history
are wanting in Goethe. But they are present in the
Saint-Simonians, whose concept had fused with the
Goethe notion.[96] That same passage from Goethe, on

---

[96] On August 11, 1832, within a few days after the notebook translation
just mentioned, Carlyle made another notebook entry that shows influence of the Goethe passage. And it faintly suggests something else. The
entry runs thus: " Politics confuse me—what my duties are therein? As
yet I have *stood apart* [Carlyle's italics], and till quite new aspects of the
matter turn up, shall continue to do so. The battle is not between Tory
and Radical (that is but like other battles); but between believer and
unbeliever." (Froude, *Thomas Carlyle . . . 1795-1835,* II, 249.) The
last sentence of this passage connects it unquestionably with Goethe.
Also the second sentence connects it with Goethe,—that is, recalls some
advice that Goethe had written Carlyle nearly two years before (October
17, 1830). That trusted guide had replied thus to Carlyle's request for
his opinion on the Saint-Simonians: " Von der Société St. Simonienne
bitte Sich fern zu halten " (*Correspondence between Goethe and Carlyle,*
p. 225). Taking up the subject again (January 22, 1831) Carlyle had
answered: " I have every disposition to follow your advice, and stand
apart from them . . ." (*ibid.,* pp. 258-259). Now, in the summer of
1832, as politics and social problems became increasingly attractive to
Carlyle's thought and as he became increasingly puzzled as to what role
he should play in his own era of political and social reform, his notebook entry—brief as it is—is suggestive. Brief and elusive as the hint
is, the entry suggests that Goethe's advice had laid a shadow of restraint
upon Carlyle's inclinations towards the Saint-Simonians. And, more
important in this discussion, it suggests that—opposed as Goethe and the
Saint-Simonians were to each other in social and political theory—they
were associated, in Carlyle's mind, with respect to a concept some parts
of which they held in common. That is, in Carlyle's mind the organic and

alternate epochs of belief and unbelief, which Carlyle
had translated during the summer in his notebook, was
used again by October 15th in the essay on Diderot.[97]
It was put at the end of the essay and was there
assigned to " the Thinker of our time."

A few pages earlier in the same essay, " Diderot,"
occurs a closely related passage, calling Diderot a
denier, one who denied the sacredness in man. " We
behold in him the notable extreme of a man guiding
himself with the least spiritual Belief that thinking man
perhaps ever had." [98]   And still elsewhere in the " Diderot " occur two statements that, though they do not
illustrate the whole of Carlyle's concept of historical
periodicity, show several points that are not in the
Goethe passage but that are in the doctrine of the
Saint-Simonians.

> . . . this epoch of the Eighteenth or Philosophe-century
> was properly the End; the End of a Social System; which
> for above a thousand years had been building itself to-
> gether, and, after that, had begun, for some centuries (as
> human things all do), to moulder down.

> . . . a torch-and-crowbar period of quick rushing-down
> and conflagration, was this of the *Siècle de Louis Quinze*
> . . . . We behold the business of pulling down, or at least
> of assorting the rubbish, still go resolutely on, all over
> Europe: here and there some traces of a new foundation,
> of new building-up, may now also to the eye of Hope,
> disclose themselves.[99]

Calling the Eighteenth Century the end of a social
system—a system that was the product of over a thou-

critical epochs of the Saint-Simonians had fused with Goethe's epochs of
belief and doubt. This notebook entry of August 11th by itself would
of course not be conclusive evidence. It is merely a minute index pointing, with the more substantial evidence that we have seen and shall see,
to the fact that Carlyle had fused elements from the two layers of
Goethean and Saint-Simonian thought.

[97] *Essays*, III, 248.   [98] *Ibid.*, III, 235.   [99] *Ibid.*, III, 179-180.

sand years of construction and which, according to the law of history, had been some centuries mouldering down—seems Saint-Simonian. The " torch-and-crowbar period " is much like the destructive critical epoch of the Saint-Simonians. And the traces of a new foundation, of a new social organization, rising out of the old ruins, suggest the palingenesia of the French Socialists.

The same notion—that destruction must be followed by social re-birth—occurs in " Cagliostro," which was finished by March 21, 1833. And " Cagliostro " contains several other elements that recall the Saint-Simonian concept of history. The late Eighteenth Century is characterized as the " very age of impostors . . . and quackeries of all colours and kinds." It was a time of economic distress and decay of moral principle: the

stertorous last fever-sleep of our European world . . . . So too, when the old Roman world, the measure of its iniquities being full,[100] was to expire, and (in still bitterer agonies)

---

[100] The diction here reminds one a little of Fichte's " *Stand der vollendeten Sündhaftigkeit*," the third epoch of the five characterized in Fichte's first lecture on *Die Grundzüge des gegenwärtigen Zeitalters* (see *Fichte's sämmtliche Werke*, ed. J. H. Fichte, Leipzig, 1845, Bd. VII, pp. 11-12). At least once later, in *Frederick*, Carlyle used diction like Fichte's. But opinion is divided as to whether he actually had read this work by Fichte. I have found no positive evidence that he had read it (see " Carlyle and the German Philosophy Problem during the Year 1826-1827," *PMLA*, L [1935], 821-824). Even if he had read the work, he would have found in it the metaphysical approach to history, instead of the sociological one. For example, Lecture I of Fichte's work stipulates that the historian's approach must be deductive: his method must be absolutely *a priori*; he must pay no respect whatever to experience. Such a metaphysical method was distasteful to Carlyle, as it was to the Saint-Simonians. However, Carlyle is so eclectic in his thought—fuses such antipathetic sources and tendencies—that one cannot afford to be dogmatic. It is a well-known fact that Fichte's lectures *Über das Wesen des Gelehrten* did heavily influence Carlyle's concept of Hero and hence his philosophy of change in history. But, even in *Heroes*, while using Fichte as his text and even while adopting Fichte's phraseology, Carlyle altered Fichte's meaning very greatly. That is, he adopted Fichte's meta-

be born again, had they not . . . False Christs enough,—
before a REDEEMER arose! [101]

Writing as if in the decades just before the French
Revolution, Carlyle exclaims:

old Feudal Europe has fallen a-dozing to die! Her next
awakening will be . . . with the stern Avatar of DEMO-
CRACY, hymning its world-thrilling birth- and battle-song in
the distant West;— therefrom to go out conquering and to
conquer, till it have made the circuit of all the Earth, and
old dead Feudal Europe is born again (after infinite pangs!)
into a new Industrial one.[102]

Thus Carlyle has gone one step further than in " Characteristics." He now points out that Democracy is only
a transition between old Feudalism and new Industrialism.[103] Just what he meant by *Industrialism*—the
new social organization for a new historical period—we
cannot now examine. But we must remark that
Dunoyer, Carlyle's first informant about the Saint-
Simonians, had used the term *Industrialism* as the name
of their social philosophy.[104] During these months,

physically arrived-at dicta to point what Carlyle at least believed to be,
and advertized as, Nineteenth Century sociological, or *a posteriori*,
methodology in history.

[101] *Essays,* III, 271.

[102] *Ibid.,* III, 270.

[103] Another comment upon the impermanence of democracy occurs in
Carlyle's letter to Mill a month later: " Democracy (like enough without
either Lords or King) at no great distance from us, as from all Europe;
and then? It is very doubtful to me whether the best possible Reformed Parliament, made of the best possible men, could *govern* in our
old world.—Nay, is not Democracy and Reformed Parliament essentially
the solemn declaration that there is *no* Government, that every man
governs himself? " (*Letters of Thomas Carlyle to . . . Mill, . . . Sterling and . . . Browning,* p. 49 [April 18, 1833]. The thought here resembles the Saint-Simonian notion that the social organization has been
destroyed and that democracy and liberalism are mere egoism.

[104] *Two Note Books,* p. 113. It is interesting to note that, during the
middle twenties of the century, there seems to have been a sort of feud

when Carlyle was moving nearer and nearer to his great work on the French Revolution, any comment showing his interpretation of the Revolution is important. Here, in " Cagliostro," he characterizes the Revolution as the burner-up, the destroyer.[105] But, as we have just seen, that destruction is only a clearing of the ground for a new growth.

Finally, in the same work, " Cagliostro," Carlyle makes some interesting statements concerning four manners of reading or interpreting universal history. He puts them into the mouth of his fantastic Sauerteig. They may have some remote bearing on the question we are discussing.

'. . . out of all imaginable elements, awakening all imaginable moods of heart and soul, . . . ever contradictory yet ever coalescing, is that mighty world-old Rhapsodia of Existence page after page (generation after generation), and chapter (or epoch) after chapter, poetically put together! This is what some one names " the grand sacred Epos, or Bible of World-History; infinite in meaning as the Divine Mind it emblems; wherein he is wise that can read here a line, and there a line." . . . What is all History, and all Poesy, but a deciphering somewhat thereof, out of that mystic heaven-written Sanscrit . . . ? . . . Here also I will observe, that the *manner* in which men read this same Bible is, like all else, proportionate to their stage of culture . . .   First, and among the earnest Oriental nations, it was read wholly like a Sacred Book; most clearly by the most earnest, those wondrous Hebrew Readers . . . . But, again, in how different a style was that other Oriental reading of the Magi; of Zerdusht, or whoever it was

between Dunoyer and the Saint-Simonians. In addition to Dunoyer's article on " Industrialisme " (*Revue encyclopédique*, XXXIII [February, 1827], 368-394), see *Le Producteur*, II, 158-170, and 451-464, for P. J. Rouen's hostile review of a work by Dunoyer. However, *Le Producteur's* hostility did not extend to *Revue encyclopédique* (see *Le Producteur*, II, 429-432, and IV, 350-355).

[105] *Essays*, III, 274.

that first so opened the matter?   Gorgeous semisensual Grandeurs and Splendours: . . .—of which, . . . turned mostly into lies, a quite late reflex, in those Arabian Tales and the like, still leads captive every human heart.   Look, thirdly, at the earnest West, and that Consecration of the Flesh, which stept forth life-lusty, radiant, smiling-earnest, in immortal grace, from under the chisel and stylus of old Greece . . . .—Of which three antique manners of reading, our modern manner, you will remark, has been little more than imitation: for always, indeed, the West has been rifer of doers than of speakers.   The Hebrew manner has had its echo in our Pulpits and choral aisles; the Ethnic Greek and the Arabian in numberless mountains of Fiction . . . . Till now at last, by dint of iteration and reiteration through some ten centuries, all these manners have grown obsolete, wearisome, meaningless; . . .—and so now, well-nigh in total oblivion of the Infinitude of Life . . . we wait, in hope and patience, for some *fourth* manner of anew convincingly announcing it.[106]

In that passage from Sauerteig, Carlyle seems to be speculating upon, among other things, something akin to the historical periods that we have already seen. But even with the addition of the Hebrew period, with which Goethe rather than the Saint-Simonian Society deals, the passage is far from the concept of historical periodicity in the Saint-Simonians, in Goethe, or elsewhere in Carlyle. The nearest approach to the four manners here discussed is the concept of the Four Kings, which Carlyle had put into Teufelsdröckh's commentary on Goethe's *Das Mährchen* in 1832. It will be well to remember that in 1833 Carlyle was experiencing great confusion of thought.[107] Apparently, as

[106] *Ibid.*, III, 250-253.

[107] Strangely enough the essay " On History Again," which we can date only approximately as late 1832 or early 1833, contains nothing significant about periodicity. The leading topics in this short—and apparently incomplete—discussion of history are the practical problems of compression and selection, which are based upon a notion of the sur-

I have endeavored to show elsewhere, for some months he had been attempting to go beyond his old position and to formulate not a philosophy of history, but a fusion of history, art, and religion.[108]

If there are no specific references to the Saint-Simonians in the articles that he wrote for publication between his departure from London in 1832 and his return to London in 1834, that fact may be partly accounted for by their scandalous proceedings, by their period of monastic retreat, by the court-trial in the summer of 1832, and by the consequent disruption of the Society. Even while he was evaluating Goethe as the victorious reconciler of the distracted and disorganized elements of life, the Saint-Simonians were undergoing humiliation. But Carlyle's letters prove that the Saint-Simonians were strongly in his mind at least once during even those busy early months. In the spring of 1832, when Mill wrote him about the Society in retirement at Menilmontant, doing menial services for one another,[109] Carlyle pitied them and dwelt upon the extenuating circumstances of their defeat.

The poor Saint-Simonians! [Carlyle responded to Mill]. Figure Duveyrier, with waiter's apron emptying slop-pails,—for the salvation of the world. But so it is: many must try, before one can succeed: what too are we but trials; seekers, smoothing the way for others, who likewise

vival of the greatest. The notion of the survival of the greatest and worthiest is found, as Professor Harrold shows (*Carlyle and German Thought: 1819-1834*, p. 176), in Goethe's " Israel in der Wüste." See also *supra*, p. 101, note 94a.

[108] For the development of this fusion, see my *Carlyle's Fusion of Poetry, History, and Religion by 1834* (Chapel Hill, University of North Carolina Press, 1938).

[109] *The Letters of John Stuart Mill* (ed. by H. S. R. Elliot, London, 1910), I, 30-31 (May 29, 1832). See also Froude, *Thomas Carlyle . . . 1795-1835*, II, 225 (July 31, 1832), for Carlyle's statement that he gets from Mill information about the Saint-Simonians.

will not wholly *find?* The men [the Saint-Simonians] are to be honoured and loved in this, that they have dared to be men, as they could, tho' the *Gig* [the institutions and respectabilities of contemporary society] should break altogether down with them, and nothing remain for it but bare soles. Such a feat is too hard for above one in ten thousand; yet for all except very fortunate men, it is the first condition of true worth. As to the Saint-Simonian Sect, it seems nearly sure to die with the existing " Father of Humanity " [i. e., Enfantin]; but in his hands it may hold together, and do much indirect good. While " the Fancy " [i. e., the sporting-class] remain in England unwhipt and without hemp-mallets in their hands, let the Saint-Simonians remain unlaughed at.[110]

Thus Carlyle honored the Saint-Simonians for having dared to break with the worn-out social organization of their time. Although he now thought that the Sect would not be permanent, up until the time of the court-trial he supposed that it might for a while hold together and continue to do much indirect good. But, in the fall, after Mill had written him of the trial, he accepted without demur the disruption of the Society.

I owe you many thanks for your few sentences on that matter of their Trial, which I had elsewhere inquired after in vain. If you have any pamphlets, books, or even newspaper-leaves about it to lend me, I should still be glad of them. I sometimes even think of writing about it,—in some dialect or other; had I materials. Enfantin becomes quite intelligible to me from my knowledge of Edward Irving. The Enthusiast nowise excludes the Quack; nay rather (especially in such times as these) presupposes him. Do you know where Gustave d'Eichthal is? Or what Duveyrier makes of himself in prison? Which *is* their prison? [111]

[110] *Letters of Thomas Carlyle to . . . Mill, . . . Sterling and . . . Browning,* p. 9 (June 16, 1832).
[111] *Ibid.,* p. 19 (October 16, 1832).

Evidently Carlyle, even in the face of the public humiliation of the Society, still had some intention of writing about Saint-Simonism as a sign of the times. And if he had come to regard Enfantin as an enthusiastic quack, he still felt a lively personal sympathy toward his two former missionary friends.

During the year 1833 his intellectual curiosity concerning the Saint-Simonians continued, and his deep personal interest in Gustave d'Eichthal continued and even increased. Although Enfantin's highly questionable developments caused Carlyle to applaud Gustave's break with Le Père, Carlyle still believed there was good in some of the Saint-Simonian doctrines. For example, he said that Harriet Martineau could learn much from them.[112] And he was himself still planning to write on the Society, even though he lacked some of the materials for his article. Therefore he reminded Mill not to forget "the Saint-Simonian Books." [112] Mill, sometimes in London and sometimes in Paris, did not forget the books containing records of the court-trials of the Saint-Simonians. Neither did he forget Carlyle, now in Edinburgh for a stay of several months. Nor did John Carlyle, in Rome, forget his brother.[113] Both of them—but chiefly Mill—supplied Carlyle with whatever they could learn of the doings of the Saint-Simonians. Early in the spring of 1833 Mill wrote him a detailed report and one or two striking generalizations about the Society. The generalizations are especially important for us to notice. Mill believed that the Saint-Simonian Society was the only spiritual fruit of the

---

[112] *Ibid.*, pp. 40-41 (February 22, 1833).

[113] John Carlyle reported that Gustave d'Eichthal, whom he had met in Rome, was uncommunicative concerning Saint-Simonism, was dispirited, and seemed considerably bewildered (*ibid.*, p. 45 [March 21, 1833]).

Revolution of 1830. The Society, he said, had set afloat the only new ideas—new to Frenchmen—that had been launched in France during that era of the Second Revolution; and Saint-Simon, himself, was, " for a Frenchman," a really great man. Enfantin too could have been a sort of great man, Mill thought; but the other Saint-Simonians were mere amplifiers and redactors of the thoughts of their two leaders.[114] With those generalizations by Mill, Carlyle agreed, adding that he feared Duveyrier was " but a kind of Dilettante." [115] That comment on Duveyrier, possibly a concession to Mill's estimate of the disciples, leaves Gustave the only one of the Saint-Simonians with whom Carlyle's sympathy remained unimpaired by the spring of 1833. Carlyle's agreement with Mill on the importance and on the degree of originality of the Saint-Simonian leaders is a noteworthy point. For, though the Saint-Simonian publications had been important in the development of both Mill's and Carlyle's thought, little of the gleam that had once surrounded the Society now remained.

In the early summer, 1833, Carlyle's reading of the record of the Saint-Simonian trial called forth some comments not only on the Saint-Simonians of the 1830 Days but on the Revolutionists of 1789. The record of the trial—along with two letters, one from Duveyrier and one from Gustave d'Eichthal—had been sent by Mill.[116] And on June 13th Carlyle wrote Mill his thanks. The Trial,[117] he said, was better than any drama he had

---

[114] *The Letters of John Stuart Mill,* I, 43-44 (April 11 and 12, 1833).

[115] *Letters of Thomas Carlyle to . . . Mill, . . . Sterling and . . . Browning,* pp. 51-52 (April 18, 1833).

[116] *The Letters of John Stuart Mill,* I, 40; 43-44.

[117] Probably *Procès en la cour d'assises de la Seine, les 27 et 28 aôut 1832* (Paris, à la librairie Saint-Simonienne, 1832). This book of 405 pages has as its general title *Religion Saint-Simonienne.* Under the same general title was published also the 105-page *Procès en Police correction-*

seen for years; and it, read along with Gustave's letter, constituted at once a chimera and a truth. In the light of those documents he found that his love for Gustave had increased. Once Gustave had been separated from the fantastic crudities of the Sect, there would be hope, Carlyle said, for his future. At the same time that Carlyle called the peculiarities of the Sect exceedingly lamentable, he admitted they were deeply interesting.[118] Possibly even more important to the student of Carlyle's intellectual development is the comment upon French character in general, for Carlyle was rapidly moving, through his connection with the Saint-Simonians, toward his interpretation of the great French Revolution. He was puzzled, he said, by the French character, as seen in the last two generations and in the last two revolutions—the generation of 1789 and the generation of 1830. Was it not, he wondered, very barren, very lean? And he expatiated thus upon his own question:

Never was a nation worse prepared with individual strength or light of any kind for a bursting asunder of all old bounds and habits; the old Sansculottes had only the strength to kill and to die: and then these new figures, with their Bankrupt Projector of a God-man, and all this of the *femme libre,* and their inability to speak *till* she appear (and *vote,* by ballot or otherwise)—did the world often witness the like? [119]

Again, in that comment, Carlyle may have been glancing back at Mill's earlier generalizations about the Saint-Simonians. But, in his interpretation of the Sans-

nelle, le 19 Octobre 1832). (Paris, à la librairie Saint-Simonienne, 1832.) Both accounts are included in the last volume (XLVII) of *Oeuvres de Saint-Simon et d'Enfantin* (Paris, 1878).
    [118] *Letters of Thomas Carlyle to . . . Mill, . . . Sterling and . . . Browning*, pp. 57-58.
    [119] *Ibid.*, p. 58 (June 13, 1833).

culottes of the first French Revolution, he was echoing the analysis presented by the Saint-Simonians themselves in their early seances, which stressed philosophy of history instead of messianism and femininism.

At several times during the late summer and the fall of 1833 the Saint-Simonians were in Carlyle's mind, for various reasons. August brought him, in the visit of Emerson, a beautiful reminder of his old friendship with the well-loved disciple, Gustave d'Eichthal. Indirectly, through Gustave's good offices, Emerson was introduced first in London and then at Craigenputtock. Gustave had sent him to Mill for a direct introduction to Carlyle.[120] But of Gustave, Emerson could report very little. Two days later, Carlyle directed John Carlyle to seek, divert, and cheer the bewildered disciple who could not tell where to find his master; to tell him of Carlyle's affectionate esteem; and to invite him to visit Craigenputtock. Furthermore, Carlyle wished a report on him as John came back through Paris.[121] And to Mill, Carlyle wrote much the same:

I feel much interest in poor Gustave: of all the Saint-Simonians *he* probably was the truest, his disappointment will be the deepest. Bring me home news of him, if possible; convey to him also my friendliest wishes, if you have opportunity.[122]

And in the fall, before Mill set out for France, Carlyle asked him again not to forget the d'Eichthals.[123] If that request was motivated by personal feelings, the

[120] *Letters of John Stuart Mill*, I, 57, 60; *Letters of Thomas Carlyle, 1826-1836*, pp. 371-372; *Lettres de Thomas Carlyle à sa mère* (tr. E. Masson, Paris, 1907), p. 167.
[121] *Letters of Thomas Carlyle, 1826-1836*, pp. 371-372 (August 27, 1833).
[122] *Letters of Thomas Carlyle to . . . Mill, . . . Sterling and . . . Browning*, p. 67 (September 10, 1833).
[123] *Ibid.*, p. 82 (October 28, 1833).

inquiry concerning Enfantin's whereabouts, in the same letter, probably had a different meaning. For Carlyle was again entertaining the idea of writing an essay on the Saint-Simonians.[124] But when in November he heard that they were again active, " giving missionary lectures of a most questionable sort in London," he appears to have given up for the last time all intentions of writing upon them.[125] Henceforth his interest in the contemporary affairs of the Saint-Simonians seems to have been based entirely upon personal sympathy with Gustave d'Eichthal. And so far as the records show, even that interest was short-lived.

In tracing out materials concerning the Diamond Necklace, which by October 1st he had practically decided upon as his next paper-topic,[126] Carlyle contracted his last debt of gratitude to the d'Eichthal family. And, at the same time, he received the last written report on the Saint-Simonians from Mill. Mill's report and Adolphe d'Eichthal's favour are closely connected. As before mentioned, when Mill was about to pay his autumn visit to France, Carlyle had asked him to gather information about the Saint-Simonians. And he had asked Mill further to seek out some details about the Necklace Affair, purchase some books, and reconnoiter concerning living-conditions in Paris. The last-named request was made in view of Carlyle's growing plan to study the actual scene of the great Revolution. Late in November, Mill, now back in London, reported on his Paris visit. He reported many facts about the former Saint-Simonians and the courses they were taking. He

[124] See also *Letters of Thomas Carlyle, 1826-1836,* pp. 376-377 (October 1, 1833).
[125] Froude, *Thomas Carlyle . . . 1795-1835,* II, 307 (November 18, 1833, letter to John Carlyle).
[126] *Letters of Thomas Carlyle, 1826-1836,* pp. 376-377 (October 1, 1833, letter to John Carlyle).

believed that they had in the past done much good and that they were still doing some good. Most of them, he thought, had retained from the Saint-Simonian doctrines about all that was good and true, and had dropped the rest.[127] In discharging the other commissions for Carlyle, Mill had enlisted the help of Gustave d'Eichthal's brother, Adolphe. Adolphe, delighted in the hopes of further connection with the Scot whom he had met in London, had searched out books and had sent Carlyle's questions on the *Collier* case to several persons whom he thought likely to be informed. One set of answers, from a Baron Darnay, who had been present at the *Collier* trial, Mill had been able to bring back with him, and had forwarded the paper to Carlyle in Scotland.[128] In this Baron's paper and in a later packet of documents on the *Collier*, direct from Adolphe in Paris, Carlyle found much that was helpful to him in his new study.[129] And the new study in turn helped him on his way toward *The French Revolution*.

But by the time Carlyle left Scotland for good in the spring of 1834, he had lost or broken the friendly connections with the Saint-Simonian group. Those connections, already for some time before his departure, had been continued only through the aid of Mill, John Carlyle, and Emerson. A few months after taking up permanent residence in London, he mentioned to Emerson, as if of merely incidental interest, the fact that Gustave d'Eichthal had gone to Greece.[130] And by the autumn of 1834 he did not know Duveyrier's address in

---

[127] *The Letters of John Stuart Mill,* I, 75-76 (November 25, 1833).
[128] *Ibid.,* I, 72.
[129] *Letters of Thomas Carlyle to . . . Mill, . . . Sterling and . . . Browning,* pp. 87 (December 17, 1833) and 97 (February 22, 1834).
[130] *Correspondence of Carlyle and Emerson, 1834-1872* (ed. C. E. Norton, Boston, Osgood, 1883), I, 25-26 (August 12, 1834).

Paris.[131]   His friendly connections with the Saint-Simonians, like his long-entertained project of writing an essay upon the Society, had given way as he became more and more engrossed in the French Revolution.

The period of some three years from *Sartor* to the beginning of *The French Revolution* shows much important evidence upon Carlyle's relation to the Saint-Simonians and to Saint-Simonian thought.   In *Sartor*, he quoted from and referred to the Society; stated the law of progressive periodic mutation; characterized the alternate epochs as epochs of faith and epochs of denial; and stated clearly the concept of transition between periods, using the term *palingenesia* as well as the symbol of the phoenix.   Though he dealt with only a recent part of European history, he dealt with that part in a way closely similar to the Saint-Simonian analysis: he insisted upon the virtual non-existence of the old society, condemned mere independence and freedom, and regarded liberals as destructives useful only as clearers of ground.   And he looked forward, for the future, to a palingenesia of society under a government of the wisest.   In " Characteristics," which contains a slightly veiled reference to the religious pretensions of the Society, he again stressed periodicity and the palingenetic transition between periods.   His discussion of epochs shows excellently the fusion of Goethean thought and Saint-Simonian thought.   Though his characterization of the vitally unified epochs and of the skeptical epochs is in general related to the Goethe *Glauben*-and-*Unglauben* characterization, the details go far beyond Goethe and are very similar to the Saint-Simonian characterization of organic and critical epochs.   Carlyle's designation of the various epochs in past history draws

---

[131] *Letters of Thomas Carlyle to . . . Mill, . . . Sterling and . . . Browning*, p. 103 (early September, 1834).

upon Goethe as well as upon the Saint-Simonians; but his discussion of the organizing schemata unifying the vital epochs again goes far beyond Goethe. And his presentation of his main interest—the present skeptical epoch, verging toward an affirmative epoch—shows great reliance upon the Saint-Simonians. In the essay on Boswell's *Johnson,* he again quoted from the Saint-Simonians; and he characterized the Age of Johnson in terms that recall the Saint-Simonian characterization of the last critical epoch. During this time, Carlyle's high regard for the Saint-Simonian philosophy of history may have been reinforced by the attitude of his London associates, John Mill and the *Fraser's* group. Meanwhile too he became a regular and eager reader of the daily *Globe,* which was the last of the Saint-Simonian publications (except the Trial) that he is known to have studied. And early in his visit to London his letters and journal contain favorable references to the Society. But about the time of " Characteristics," possibly because of Enfantin's vagaries in matters of religion and sex, Carlyle's attitude toward the current activities of the Society seems to have changed to one of uneasiness and even of disparagement. And his short, though pleasant, contact with the Society's missionaries in London left no gain except in his personal regard for those particular apostles. His return to Scotland, the rapid series of events that led to the disruption of the Society, and the shock that resulted to Carlyle from the death of Goethe contributed to the curtailment of his references to the Saint-Simonians during the middle half of 1832. During those six months, in Carlyle's various published comments on Goethe, the echoes of the Saint-Simonian concept of history, though notable, are not as numerous or as significant as the striking resemblances found in *Sartor* and " Charac-

teristics." And the *Glauben-Unglauben* passage from
Goethe becomes more prominent than ever before, lacking as it does, however, many of the elements of periodicity that Carlyle retained. Goethe's doctrine had become so thoroughly fused with the more inclusive Saint-
Simonian concept that Carlyle either could not or
would not distinguish its short-comings. Furthermore,
another basis for Carlyle's emphasis, in 1832, on the
artist Goethe was the fact that Carlyle was then attempting to work out, not a philosophy of history, but
an artistic expression of that philosophy of history.
Nevertheless, in " Diderot " he echoed, as he had echoed
in " Johnson," the Saint-Simonian characterization of
the Eighteenth Century critical epoch. Notwithstanding preoccupation with other subjects and in spite of
the humiliation of the Society, Carlyle's correspondence
shows that he retained his warm personal sympathy at
least for Gustave d'Eichthal, and kept his intellectual
curiosity concerning the Saint-Simonian thought and its
effect upon the times. He agreed with some of Mill's
generalizations about the importance of Saint-Simonian
thought. And he still intended writing upon the Society,
which Mill called the only spiritual fruit of the Revolution of 1830 and which had helped both Mill and Carlyle to interpret the Revolution of 1789. But the Revolution of 1789 gradually absorbed Carlyle's attention.
After he had given up his plan of writing an essay on
the Saint-Simonians, high personal regard still existed
for a while between him and the d'Eichthal brothers.
Acting through Mill, Gustave provided Emerson his
viaticum to Craigenputtock and Adolphe furnished material for *The Diamond Necklace*. And Carlyle's sympathy and gratitude were relayed back to the brothers
through John Mill and John Carlyle. Then, as shades
of the Bastille closed upon the imagination of Carlyle,

he lost even this connection with his former friends among the extinguished sect.   Long before *The French Revolution* was published, all personal communication between the Saint-Simonians and Carlyle was a thing of the past, like the fecundating tracts that had been sent in packets to Craigenputtock and like the revealing responses that had gone back to Paris in letters during the *Sartor* months.   But the influence that the Saint-Simonian thought had exerted upon Carlyle's thought was to remain in midst of other woe, and play a part in his later utterances.

CHAPTER V

FROM *The French Revolution* TO *Heroes* (1835-1841)

Like the period of three years covered in the preceding chapter, the period of six years to be considered in the present chapter shows very important uses of the Saint-Simonian concept of historical periodicity. However, two differences are worth noting now. The preceding chapter gave evidence derived from both the familiar writings and the more formal utterances; the present chapter deals with evidence derived almost entirely from the more formal, or studied, utterances. And instead of the problem's being complicated, as in the preceding chapter, by a changing attitude on Carlyle's part toward the current activities of the Saint-Simonian Society, the present chapter is simplified by the fact that, before *The French Revolution* was begun, the current activities of the sect had ceased.

Most of the evidence in the present chapter comes from four works of widely varied scope. In the fall of 1834, after long and gradual preparation, Carlyle began *The French Revolution*; and he finished it in a little more than two years, by mid-January 1837. Of the four sets of annual lectures that he delivered from 1837 to 1840, only two sets were published: the lectures of 1838, from notes taken by a hearer; the lectures of 1840, by Carlyle himself, in 1841. And *Chartism*, of 1839, the year between those lectures, shows the strong social drift that in later years led to *Past and Present* and *Latter-Day Pamphlets*.

Though in *The French Revolution* Carlyle makes no

specific allusion to the Saint-Simonians, he shows the philosophy of history toward which they and Goethe had led him. Believing the Revolution the final destruction of feudalism, he considers that destruction only a phase of the great law of historical periodicity.

All things are in revolution; in change from moment to moment, which becomes sensible from epoch to epoch: in this Time-World of ours there is properly nothing else but revolution and mutation, and even nothing else conceivable![1]

He divides this long process of world-history into a succession of alternate epochs—epochs of growth and epochs of destruction,—in which ideals, schemata, world-theories, or directive principles develop and then decay.

How . . . Ideals [such as kingship] do realise themselves; and grow, wondrously, from amid the incongruous ever-fluctuating chaos of the Actual: this is what World-History, if it teach anything, has to teach us. How they grow; and, after long stormy growth, bloom out mature, supreme; then quickly (for the blossom is brief) fall into decay; sorrowfully dwindle; and crumble down, or rush down, noisily or noiselessly disappearing.[2]

That is the doctrine of periodic mutation that Carlyle had used for several years.

In characterizing the alternate epochs of growth and epochs of destruction, he is closer to Goethe than to the Saint-Simonians. Like Goethe, he characterizes the epochs of growth as epochs of faith. He adds that the epochs of transcendent spiritual faith, the great blossoming-times of a people's culture, are brief.

[1] *The French Revolution. A History* (London, Chapman and Hall, 1898), I, 211 (1835).
[2] *Ibid.*, I, 10.

Seldom do we find that a whole People can be said to have any Faith at all; except in things it can eat and handle. Whensoever it gets any Faith, its history becomes spirit-stirring, noteworthy.[3]

And for the characterization of the opposite kind of epochs—epochs in which faith is lacking—he again goes to Goethe.

But of those decadent ages [Carlyle asks, rhetorically] in which no Ideal either grows or blossoms? When Belief and Loyalty have passed away, and only the cant and false echo of them remains; and all Solemnity has become Pageantry; and the Creed of persons in authority has become one of two things: an Imbecility or a Macchia-velism? Alas, of these ages World-History can take no notice; they have to become compressed more and more, and finally suppressed in the Annals of Mankind; blotted out as spurious,—which indeed they are.[4]

Plainly Goethean even is the doctrine of survival of the worthiest, which here occurs in germ, expressed in terms of the compression of historical annals.

Great as is Carlyle's debt to Goethe in those characterizations of the epochs of faith and lack-of-faith, his debt in tracing out the epochs in actual history is chiefly to the Saint-Simonians. However, he does not in *The French Revolution* reproduce the complete historical sketch of either of his sources. His sketch reveals both omissions and additions of positive, or faithful, epochs. The first organic epoch of the Saint-Simonians, remember, had been the early polytheistic paganism of the Greeks and Romans. And the only epoch of faith to which Goethe pointed specifically was the early age of the Hebrews. To neither of those epochs in his sources does Carlyle here refer. But the second organic

---

[3] *Ibid.*, III, 119 (by early 1837).   [4] *Ibid.*, I, 10-11.

epoch of the Saint-Simonians was the era of Catholicism and feudalism. To that epoch, he devotes considerable attention.

. . . since the time when steel Europe shook itself simultaneously at the word of Hermit Peter, and rushed towards the Sepulchre where God had lain, there was no universal impulse of Faith that one could note.[5]

In another volume, falling back again on his figure of blossom and decay, he speaks of medieval Catholicism and feudalism as lasting until the reign of Louis XIV in France.

The blossom is so brief; as of some centennial Cactus-flower, which after a century of waiting shines out for hours! Thus from the day when rough Clovis . . . had to cleave retributively the head of that rough Frank . . . forward to Louis the Grand and his *L'État c'est moi*, we count some twelve hundred years: and now this the very next Louis is dying, and so much dying with him!—Nay, thus too, if Catholicism, with and against Feudalism . . . , gave us English a Shakspeare and Era of Shakspeare, and so produced a blossom of Catholicism—it was not till Catholicism itself, so far as Law could abolish it, had been abolished here.[6]

Then he does what neither Goethe nor the Saint-Simonians had done. That is, he designates subordinate epochs of partial or national, instead of pan-European, faith. He includes in that list four different movements, in four different centuries, in four different countries: the Hussite movement in Fifteenth Century Bohemia, the Lutheran movement in Sixteenth Century Germany, the Cameronian Covenanting movement in Seventeenth Century Scotland, and the revolutionary social movement of late Eighteenth Century France.[7] But he does

[5] *Ibid.*, III, 119.   [6] *Ibid.*, I, 10.   [7] *Ibid.*, III, 119.

not elaborate the first three of those epochs of national faith. All three of them are discussed within one sentence. The last of the epochs—the French Revolution—is of course greatly elaborated in the book. But generally, as will be shown in the next paragraph, he considers the French Revolution the scene of final destruction and abolition of incredibilities, instead of a time of constructive faith. Thus much Carlyle in *The French Revolution* gives on the positive epochs of belief.

In designating negative, or decadent, epochs, he is closer to his Saint-Simonian sources. The Saint-Simonians had designated two critical epochs: the end of the Roman Empire and the end of the feudal-Catholic system. Carlyle makes only a brief allusion to the destruction of the Roman Empire, merely to point an analogy between it and the French Revolution, with respect to both the destruction and the noisy confusion that accompanied the destruction.[8] But concerning the second, or recent, decadent epoch he writes much more fully. After considering decadent epochs as epochs in which no Ideal grows or blossoms—as epochs in which belief and loyalty have passed away—he continues: " In such a decadent age, or one fast verging that way, had our poor Louis [i. e., Louis XV] been born." [9] Obviously he believes Louis' reign the end of the old period, for he comments thus on Saint-Pierre's *Paul et Virginie* and Louvet's *Chevalier de Faublas*:

Noteworthy Books; which may be considered as the last-speech of old Feudal France. . . . we will call his [i. e., Saint-Pierre's] Book the swan-song of old dying France.[10]

A hundred and fifty pages later in the same volume he again acts as choragos and comments on the stormy pageant that ensued.

[8] *Ibid.,* III, 2.   [9] *Ibid.,* I, 11.   [10] *Ibid.,* I, 60.

For as Hierarchies and Dynasties of all kinds, Theocracies, Aristocracies, Autocracies, Strumpetocracies, have ruled over the world; so it was appointed, in the decrees of Providence, that this same Victorious Anarchy, Jacobinism, Sansculottism, French Revolution, Horrors of French Revolution, or what else mortals name it, should have its turn. The 'destructive wrath' of Sansculottism: this is what we speak, having unhappily no voice for singing.

Surely a great Phenomenon: nay it is a *transcendental* one, overstepping all rules and experience; the crowning Phenomenon of our Modern Time.[11]

May 4, 1789, he considers a day like few others:

It is the baptism-day of Democracy. . . . The extreme-unction day of Feudalism! A superannuated System of Society . . . is now to die: and so, with death-throes and birth-throes, a new one is to be born.[12]

Although in this passage he says nothing concerning the Catholic religious system, he specifically mentions the feudal social and political system as the one abolished. And elsewhere, as shown in the preceding paragraph, he links feudalism and Catholicism. That is, he, like the Saint-Simonians, considers feudalism and Catholicism the schemata, or directive principles, of the second period.

The method of transition between periods is described in its connection with the French Revolution. Though he does not use the term *palingenesia,* he does use the phoenix figure to symbolize the growth of the new along with the destruction of the old.

The age of Miracles has come back! 'Behold the World-Phoenix, in fire-consummation and fire-creation: wide are her fanning wings; loud is her death melody, of battle-thunders and falling towns; skyward lashes the funeral flame, enveloping all things: it is the Death-Birth of a World!'[13]

[11] *Ibid.,* I, 212.   [12] *Ibid.,* I, 133.   [13] *Ibid.,* I, 213.

This phoenix figure, which he had elaborated at great length in *Sartor Resartus* four years earlier, contains in it, perhaps as fully as symbolic language can be expected to contain a historical doctrine, the Saint-Simonian doctrine of *palingenesis*.

In *The French Revolution,* as in " Characteristics," he insists that no one schema, or world-theory, can be final. It is the function of a critical epoch to tear to pieces the old schema, and project another and more adequate one.

Theories of Government! Such have been, and will be; in ages of decadence. Acknowledge them in their degree; as processes of Nature, who does nothing in vain; as steps in her great process. Meanwhile, what theory is so certain as this, That all theories, were they never so earnest, painfully elaborated, are, and, by the very conditions of them, must be incomplete, questionable, and even false? Thou shalt know that this Universe is, what it professes to be, an *infinite* one. . . . That a new young generation has exchanged the Sceptic Creed, *What shall I believe?* for passionate Faith in this [social contract] Gospel according to Jean Jacques is a further step in the business; and betokens much.[14]

And, further, Carlyle assumes the role of prophet and touches upon the future organization of society. To him, as to the Saint-Simonians, democracy seems inevitable,—desirable only because transitory. To them both, it is synonymous with anarchy and is only the forerunner of a more positive form of government. But to Carlyle, writing after France's July Days and England's Parliamentary Reform, the transition stage threatens to be longer and more difficult than the Saint-Simonians had believed in their best days of social and political prophecy. Writing in his first volume, 1835, on the birth-throes of democracy, Carlyle exclaims:

[14] *Ibid.,* I, 54.

What a work . . . ! . . . and from this present date, if
one might prophesy, some two centuries of it still to fight!
Two centuries; hardly less; before Democracy go through
its due, most baleful, stages of *Quack*ocracy; and a pestilent
World be burnt up, and have begun to grow green and
young again.[15]

A year later, he writes in his last volume,

Shams are burnt up; nay, what as yet is the peculiarity of
France, the very Cant of them is burnt up. The new
Realities are not yet come: ah no, only Phantasms, Paper
models, tentative Prefigurements of such![16]

And he quotes his prophecy from " Cagliostro " :

' IMPOSTURE is in flames, Imposture is burnt up. . . .
Higher, higher yet flames the Fire-Sea. . . . RESPECTABILITY,
with all her collected Gigs inflamed for funeral pyre, wailing,
leaves the Earth: not to return save under new Avatar.
Imposture how it burns, through generations: how it is
burnt up; for a time. The World is black ashes;—which,
ah, when will they grow green? ' . . . This Prophecy, we
say, has it not been fulfilled, is it not fulfilling?[17]

In the same final volume of *The French Revolution,*
he says that the Aristocracy of Feudal Parchment
having passed away, France has arrived by a natural
course at an Aristocracy of the Moneybag.

It is the course through which all European Societies are,
at this hour, travelling. Apparently a still baser sort of
Aristocracy? An infinitely baser; the basest yet known.
   In which however, there is this advantage, that, like
Anarchy itself, it cannot continue. . . .
   Meanwhile we will hate Anarchy as Death, which it is. . . .
Anarchy is destruction; a burning up, say, of Shams and
Insupportabilities; but which leaves Vacancy behind. . . .
And so Vacancy and general Abolition having come for

---

[15] *Ibid.,* I, 133.   [16] *Ibid.,* III, 322.   [17] *Ibid.,* III, 322-323.

this France, what can Anarchy do more? Let there be Order, were it under the Soldier's Sword. . . .[18]

Here in *The French Revolution,* as already earlier in " Cagliostro," is the denunciation of democracy. And such denunciation was to occupy a large place in Carlyle's social writings.

The evidence presented from *The French Revolution* in all except one point shows itself consistent with the Saint-Simonian concept of historical periodicity though not in every particular analogous to it. The doctrine of progress and necessary change, decadence following growth; the characterization of the alternate epochs of belief and skepticism (which derives directly from Goethe); the designation and description of the medieval epoch of growth and the Eighteenth Century epoch of ultimate decay and destruction; the method of transition between periods; the insistence that no schema can be final; and the conclusion that democracy and anarchy are synonymous—all these elements in *The French Revolution* are consistent with the Saint-Simonian doctrine. The characterizations of the alternate epochs of belief and unbelief, though consonant with the Saint-Simonian doctrine, are clearly dependent upon Goethe for their wording. The only point inconsistent with the Saint-Simonians is Carlyle's brief designation of national epochs of belief in the Fifteenth, Sixteenth, Seventeenth, and Eighteenth Centuries.

Two by-products of *The French Revolution* deserve some attention at this point. They are the essay on Mirabeau and the essay on Buchez and Roux's *Histoire parlementaire.* The first, " Mirabeau," was written in the summer of 1836 for Mill's *Westminster Review.* That essay as it now stands printed in Carlyle's *Works*

---

[18] *Ibid.,* III, 314-316.

contains no direct reference to the Saint-Simonians. But Carlyle's letter to Mill on July 22, 1836, suggests that something in the original manuscript had been altered by Mill. " I . . . noticed (I think) something you had changed about Saint-Simonism; here too your pencilling seemed better than the pen-work." [19] Apparently Carlyle accepted Mill's alteration and omitted the offending passage when " Mirabeau " was printed. What the passage contained we cannot tell.[20] But a specific and derogatory comment on the religious aspect of Saint-Simonism occurs in the other essay, which was published in April 1837, shortly after the appearance of *The French Revolution.* This essay, after commenting on the value of *The Parliamentary History of the French Revolution,* speaks briefly of its authors, Buchez and Roux, as men of ability and repute. Then, concerning these authors, Carlyle adds: " they once listened a little to Saint-Simon, but it was before Saint-Simonism called itself ' a religion,' and vanished in Bedlam." [21] Nothwithstanding that depreciatory attitude toward Saint-Simonian religious developments, a passage at the beginning of the essay contains several points that may echo the Saint-Simonian interpretation of history, and especially their interpretation of the French Revolution. The Revolution, says Carlyle, is the event of these modern ages. It was

A huge explosion, bursting through all formulas and customs; . . . blotting-out one may say, the very firmament

---

[19] *Letters of Thomas Carlyle to . . . Mill, . . . Sterling and . . . Browning,* p. 133.

[20] A likely place for the omitted passage to have occurred would be *Essays,* III, 406, where one now reads the words, " If any man had the ambition of building a new system of morals (not a promising enterprise, at this time of day), . . ." etc.

[21] *Essays,* IV, 7.

and skyey loadstones,—though only for a season. Once in the fifteen-hundred years such a thing was ordained to come. . . . one may perhaps reasonably feel that since the time of the Crusades, or earlier, there is no chapter of history so well worth studying.[22]

Fifteen hundred years would go back to the transition between the Roman Empire and Catholic feudalism, which the Saint-Simonians had discussed as the other great transition besides the French Revolution.

Of the four courses of lectures that Carlyle delivered from 1837 to 1840, only the two for 1838 and 1840 are published. Both published courses show Saint-Simonian influence. The earlier lectures, for 1838, were *Lectures on the History of Literature, or The Successive Periods of European Culture*. They constitute the fullest single piece of evidence on Carlyle's adoption of the Saint-Simonian scheme of European history during the past twenty-three centuries. One reason for that fullness is obvious. For the first time, and indeed the only time, in his published writings his subject-matter in this course of lectures demanded that he set forth the successive epochs of European culture, from the Greeks to his own time. And in setting them forth, he adopted, to a greater extent than in any one work before or after, the scheme of history that lay ready to his hand—the Saint-Simonian scheme.

But some departures from the Saint-Simonian treatment must be pointed out for what they are worth. (1) Carlyle goes into great detail on the various national literatures in medieval and modern times. (2) In order to include Milton in a positive, or faithful, epoch, he begins the epoch of English skepticism in the Seventeenth, rather than in the Sixteenth, or Reforma-

[22] *Ibid.*, IV, 1-2.

tion, Century. And (3) the final lecture (XII), dealing with the new era, of which Carlyle had long found traces in German literature, attempts to suggest the literary, moral, and psychological implications of recent German publications, rather than to prophesy the social and political organization of the future period.[23] However, in spite of those departures or shortcomings from the Saint-Simonian treatment, and in spite of the fact that Lecture IX (on French literature from Rabelais to Rousseau) is missing from the published versions of the lectures, the lectures of 1838 show extensive use of the Saint-Simonian concept of history.

The resemblances between the concept underlying the 1838 lectures and the Saint-Simonian concept will be presented under the first four of the usual five headings that have been employed in the earlier expositions. First will come the law of inevitable progress and the view that all schemata, or world-theories, are merely temporary; second, the characterization of the alternate epochs of belief and unbelief; third, the doctrine of phoenix-like, or palingenetic, transition between periods; and fourth, the tracing of the four epochs (two complete periods) in past history. The fifth heading—the view of the future—will not be examined here, since it is devoted to German literature rather than to European political and social developments.

In the lectures of 1838, Carlyle several times states his belief in a law governing historical change. Progress of the human mind, he says,

is really that inevitable law for man[,] to go on, and to continue to widen his investigations for thousands of years

---

[23] This turning back temporarily into his former vein of German literary interest, years after his historical and social interests had superseded it, is probably more indicative of Carlyle's financial status than of his intellectual status in 1838.

or even for millions, for there is no limit to it. Any theory of nature then is at most temporary. . . . The human soul in fact develops itself into all sorts of opinions, doctrines, which go on nearer and nearer to the truth. All theories approximate more or less to the great theory which remains itself always unknown—and in that proportion contain something which must live. . . . There is no nation, too, without progress . . . ; it appears to me to be inevitably necessary. Every philosophy that exists is destined to be embraced, melted down, as it were, into some larger philosophy, which, too, will have to suffer the same some day.²⁴

Thus Carlyle in 1838 states and re-states his belief in an inevitable law of unlimited human progress and his corollary belief that all theories of the universe, or schemata of organization, must be temporary.

The alternation of epochs through which that progress must take place—that is, the doctrine of alternating epochs of belief and unbelief—he specifically assigns to Goethe. The words that he uses, though a free translation from memory, are enough like a quotation for the editor of the lectures to put the passage in quotation marks.

" It must be noted," he [Goethe] says, " that Belief and Unbelief are two opposite principles in human nature. The theme of all human history, as far as we are able to perceive it, is the contest between these two principles." " All periods," he [Goethe] goes on to say, " in which Belief predominates, in which it is the main element, the inspiring principle of action, are distinguished by great, soul-stirring, fertile events, and worthy of perpetual remembrance. And, on the other hand, when Unbelief gets the upper hand, that age is unfertile, unproductive, and intrinsically mean, in which there is no pabulum for the Spirit of man, and no one can get nourishment for himself." This passage [continues Carlyle] is one of the most pregnant utterances ever

²⁴ *Lectures on the History of Literature,* pp. 92-93. See also a similar statement on p. 116.

delivered. . . . And this same remark is altogether true of all things whatever in this world; and it throws much light on the history of the whole world. . . .[25]

The fact that Goethe's concept of alternating epochs of belief and unbelief had long been fused with the Saint-Simonian concept, which interprets and supplements Goethe, has already been discussed. Further evidence that the two sources were fused in the lectures of 1838 will be forthcoming in the paragraphs that show how Carlyle traces the positive and negative epochs in actual history.

But before we trace the epochs in past history we must point out here briefly the method of transition between historical epochs. Again, as in *Sartor* and *The French Revolution,* he uses the phoenix-figure to symbolize the growth of the new at the same time with the destruction of the old.

. . . everything that exists in time, exists with the law of change and mortality imprinted upon it; it is the story of the Phoenix, which periodically, after a thousand years, becomes a funeral pyre of its own creation, and so out of its own ashes becomes a new Phoenix. It is the law of all things.[26]

In *Sartor,* though he several times used the term *palingenesia* for the new growth, he had elaborated the phoenix-figure to furnish the fuller connotation of both destruction and rebirth. And as has already been pointed out, this phoenix-figure excellently connotes the method of transition that the Saint-Simonians had shown.

Carlyle's tracing of the two complete periods in past European history shows unmistakable Saint-

---

[25] *Ibid.,* pp. 54.　　　　　[26] *Ibid.,* p. 185.

Simonian influence. The first period was one, he indicates, in which life was organized around " the system
of Polytheism and Paganism." [27]   That polytheistic
pagan period consisted of a vital, or believing, epoch
and a decadent, or sceptical, epoch. The epoch of belief
extended to Socrates in Greece and to Ovid in Rome.
In the genuine Pagan times, " There was . . . a *Belief*,
which was accompanied by an adjustment of themselves
towards these opinions of theirs." [28]   And before the
time of Socrates, the Greek religion did necessary
service:

The mind of the whole nation, by its means, obtained a
strength and coherence.[29] . . . But about Socrates' time
this devotional feeling had in a great measure given way.[30]
. . . the Greeks went on with their wars and everything
else most prosperously, till they became *conscious* of their
condition, till the man became solicitous after other times.
Socrates, we saw, is a kind of starting point, from which we
trace their fall into confusion and wreck of all sorts.[31]
. . . Socrates was the emblem of the decline of the Greeks.
His was the mind of the Greeks in its transition state. . . .[32]
. . . After him the nation became more and more sophis-
tical. The Greek genius lost its originality, it lost its
poetry, and gave way to the spirit of speculation.[33]
. . . Euripides . . . carried his compositions occasionally
to the very verge of disease, and displays a distinct com-
mencement of the age of speculation and scepticism.[34]

Like the Greeks, the Romans too had their epoch of
vital culture, followed by an epoch of decadence.[35]
And Carlyle insists upon a national and a temporal
distinction between the two branches of pagan polytheism. That is, ". . . the Romans had their distinct

[27] *Ibid.*, p. 53.   [30] *Ibid.*   [33] *Ibid.*, p. 32.
[28] *Ibid.*, p. 55.   [31] *Ibid.*, p. 51.   [34] *Ibid.*, p. 31.
[29] *Ibid.*, p. 32.   [32] *Ibid.*, p. 31.   [35] *Ibid.*, p. 51.

system, very different from that of the Greeks. . . ." [36]
In Rome, the vital epoch lasted until the time of Ovid.[37]
But from Ovid on, in Latin culture, " we get more and
more into self-consciousness and into scepticism. . . ." [37]
A glance back over the evidence just presented in this
paragraph shows the close correspondencies between
Carlyle and the Saint-Simonians on the pagan period.
In both the Saint-Simonians and Carlyle, we see the
same organizing principle (polytheistic paganism), the
same dates (Fifth and Fourth Centuries in Greece and
First Century B. C. in Rome), the same epoch-marking
figure in Greece (Socrates), and the same national
dichotomy (Greek and Roman). These parallels are
more than chance resemblances; they are strong
evidence of influence.

Carlyle's treatment of the second period is not quite
so closely similar in all details to the Saint-Simonian
treatment. As the classical period of polytheistic paganism ended with its sceptical epoch, there gradually
emerged a new vital epoch of a new historical period.
Medieval culture was not dark and rude, says Carlyle:

It was a great and fertile period . . . that invasion of the
barbarians and their settlement in the Roman Empire.[38]
. . . . in the Middle Ages we see the great phenomenon of
Belief gaining the victory over Unbelief.[39] . . . Thus in the
Middle Ages, being in contact with fact and reality, . . .
that is the great fact of the time, Belief! [40]

In this historical period the great directive principles
were Catholicism in religion and feudalism in politics.[41]

[36] *Ibid,.* p. 185; also p. 53.
[37] *Ibid.,* p. 48. Karkaria notes concerning the word *Ovid:* " This word
is queried in the MS." The MS referred to is Anstey's manuscript report
of Carlyle's lectures. Why the word is queried, he does not say.
[38] *Ibid.,* p. 54.   [39] *Ibid.*   [40] *Ibid.,* p. 55.   [41] *Ibid.,* p. 138.

The greatest height that Christianity ever attained was in the time of Hildebrand, the Eleventh Century. Then Catholic Christianity was pan-European, and

All Europe then was firm and unshaken in the faith.[42] . . . shortly afterward we observe the rise of a kind of feeling adverse to this spirit of harmony, which we shall by and by see get out at last into Protestantism.[43]

Before the time of Galileo's martyrdom, " Europe had split itself into all kinds of confusions and contradictions without end, in which we are still enveloped." [44] And by the time of the renaissance in England, " The old principle, Feudalism, and the other one, the Catholic religion were beginning to end. . . ." [45] For Europe at large, Luther stands as the turning point.

This speech [Luther's speech at Worms] will be forever memorable. . . . It was the beginning of things not fully developed even yet, but kindled then first into a flame which shall never be extinguished. . . .[46]

Thus much of Carlyle's lectures of 1838 designated and characterized the second vital, or faithful, epoch of European civilization—the beginning of the second historical period. That epoch, or vital phase, of the period developed with the downfall of the old poly-theistic pagan culture. It was characterized by the emergence of the Catholic religion and of feudal polity as directive principles, which for a time gave unity to all Europe. But it later gave rise to gradual disruptive developments, some of which culminated in Luther.

The disruptive developments begun in the second vital epoch eventually overbalanced and destroyed the

---

[42] *Ibid.*, p. 64.   [43] *Ibid.*, p. 70.   [44] *Ibid.*, p. 92.   [45] *Ibid.*, p. 138.
[46] *Ibid.*, p. 121-122. Karkaria reads: " kindled then just." I here follow J. Reay Greene's reading in his editions of the 1838 *Lectures* (N. Y., 1892, p. 137; London, 1892, p. 130): " kindled then first."

systems that had given them rise. The destruction con-
stitutes the second decadent, or sceptical, epoch of
European culture. Unfortunately, because of Anstey's
inability to attend Lecture IX (on " French Scepticism—Voltaire—from Rabelais to Rousseau "), it is
impossible to trace all the details in Carlyle's treatment
of the early part of this sceptical epoch in France. But
we do have Carlyle's summary of the unpublished
lecture. And the summary will suffice. It runs thus:

In our last lecture we saw the melancholy phenomenon of
a system of beliefs which had grown up for 1800 years,
and had formed during that period great landmarks of the
thought of man, crumbling down at last and dissolving
itself in suicidal ruin. And we saw one of the most
remarkable nations of men engaged in destroying: nothing
growing in the great seed-field of time. . . .[47]

From that summary he proceeds:

The two great features of French intellect were formalism
and scepticism. These became the leading intellectual
features of all the nations of that [Eighteenth] century.[48]
. . . In the eighteenth century, . . . a century of disputation, if not of complete unbelief, a century of contrariety—
here with us [in England] there was nothing but argument
to be found everywhere.[49] . . . And it was not only the
disbelievers in religion that were sceptic at that time, but
the whole system of mind was sceptic.[50]

Therefore the French Revolution, when it finally came,
was the consummation, downfall, and destruction of
scepticism.[51] It

was only a great outburst of the truth, that this world was
not a mere chimera, but a great reality. . . . Scepticism
was ended; and the way laid open to new things, whenever

[47] *Ibid.*, p. 149.
[48] *Ibid.*, p. 150.
[49] *Ibid.*, p. 151.
[50] *Ibid.*, p. 166.
[51] *Ibid.*, pp. 163, 165, 183.

they should offer.[52] . . . a priceless worth was in it. By
it the European family got its feet once more out of the
mists and clouds of logic, and got down again to a firm
footing on the ground. . . .[53] [And henceforth also] the
political world, if not better regulated, [will at least be]
. . . regulated by a reality. . . .[54]

Carlyle's interpretation of the French Revolution as
the negation of a negation will not puzzle readers of
the chapter entitled " The Everlasting No " in *Sartor*.
That is, Carlyle sees the Eighteenth Century as an
epoch of decadence in religion, philosophy, and polity.
And he, like the Saint-Simonians, interprets the French
Revolution as the final beneficial though negative
sweeping-out and burning-up of the accumulated rubbish of the old and virtually non-existent institutions.[55]
The way was now clear for the formation of the new.

   Perhaps the best summary of Carlyle's designation
and characterization of the four epochs of the two great
periods of European history for the past twenty-three
centuries is a passage from the last one of his lectures
of 1838. Part of it has already been quoted; but the
whole should be seen in one piece.

. . . everything that exists in time, exists with the law of
change and mortality imprinted upon it; it is the story of
the Phoenix, which periodically, after a thousand years,
becomes a funeral pyre of its own creation, and so out of
its own ashes becomes a new Phoenix. It is the law of all
things. Paganism, for example, in its time, produced many

---

   [52] *Ibid.*, p. 182.   [53] *Ibid.*, pp. 183-184.   [54] *Ibid.*, p. 184.
   [55] When Carlyle, the next May (1839) in his fifth lecture on " The
Revolutions of Modern Europe," came to discuss the French Revolution,
an auditor reported that he " considers the French Revolution, much and
bitter fault as he has to find with it, as a consummation of Protestantism
in that respect [i. e., in protesting against only pretended beliefs]." R. H.
Shepherd, *Memoirs of the Life and Writings of Thomas Carlyle* (London,
W. H. Allen and Company, 1881), I, 208.

great things, brave and noble men, till it at last came to fall and crumble away into a mere disputatious philosophy. And so down to the Protestant system. For the middle ages in this respect answered to the heroic ages of old Greece: and as Homer had lived, so Dante lived. Similarly the destruction of the Roman system of Paganism, (for the Romans had their distinct system, very different from that of the Greeks), like the introduction of Protestantism, was followed by its own period of Werterism, a kind of blind struggle in it against the evils that lay around it, and ending at last in what was infinitely more terrific than any French Revolution, that wild in-bursting of all barbarous peoples into the old world . . . , the awfullest period ever known. And just so in later times the French Revolution . . . ; this, I say, is little less remarkable while it lasts, until there is found force enough in society to subdue it.[56]

In those lectures of 1838, Carlyle applies to the past twenty-three centuries a concept of historical periodicity that is more nearly complete than in any other single work by Carlyle. The elements tally well with the Saint-Simonian teachings: the philosophy of progress through periodic change, the Goethean concept of alternating epochs of belief and unbelief (which could as well be called organic and critical epochs), the designation and tracing of all four of the epochs—two of each sort—in the two full historical periods, the phoenix-doctrine of transition between periods, and the interpretation of the French Revolution as the negation of a negation.

At the end of 1839, between the lectures on the history of literature and those on heroes, Carlyle wrote *Chartism*. In this work the concept of history is by no means as explicit as in the lectures of the year before. He does not use Goethe's belief-unbelief characterization or the Saint-Simonian organic-critical characterization of epochs. But obviously he has in mind the concept

[56] *Lectures on the History of Literature*, p. 185.

that underlay those characterizations. When he says *Ideal*, he apparently means credible directive principle, or schema. After admitting that never, even in the most perfect feudal age, did the Actual become the Ideal, he continues:

> And yet so long as an Ideal (any soul of Truth) does, in never so confused a manner, exist and work within the Actual, it is a tolerable business. Not so, when the Ideal has entirely departed, and the Actual owns to itself that it has no Idea, no soul of Truth any longer: at that degree of imperfection human things cannot continue living; they are obliged to alter or expire, when they attain to that.[57]

The passage just quoted implies, and presumably means, the alternation of (1) epochs in which the current basic ideals, beliefs, or schemata are able to interpret life adequately, and (2) epochs in which the schemata are inadequate. And, as he had several times done in earlier years, Carlyle attempts to drive, in the figurative language of seasons, his notion of alternating epochs of growth and decay. The figurative passage is attributed to Sauerteig: " 'Long stormy spring-time, wet contentious April, winter chilling the lap of very May; but at length the season of Summer does come. . . . all things will have their time.' "[58]   The six Saxon centuries, he says, were the spring-time of England;[59] the Elizabethan era was the " ' spiritual flower-time.' "[60]

' In trees, men, institutions, creeds, nations, in all things extant and growing in this Universe, we may note such vicissitudes and budding-times. Moreover there are spiritual budding-times; and then also there are physical, appointed to nations.
  ' Thus in the middle of that poor calumniated Eighteenth Century, see once more! Long winter again past, the dead-

---

[57] *Essays*, IV, 165.
[58] *Ibid.*, IV, 180.
[59] *Ibid.*, IV, 172.
[60] *Ibid.*, IV, 180-181.

seeming tree proves to be living, to have been always living; after motionless times, every bough shoots forth on the sudden, very strangely: [this time with mechanical inventions and manufactories, which when well seen are as] beautiful as magic dreams. . . .' [61]

Thus in *Chartism* he again distinguishes between the eras in which the actual is informed by a credible ideal and the eras in which the ideal is non-existent or incredible. And in figurative language he points to the re-birth method of transition between eras. Though he discusses England from early medieval times to his own century, as having an epoch of growth followed by an epoch of decay, and suggests that both epochs are organic manifestations of a historical and natural law, he does not touch upon the manifestations of that law in the classical civilizations. From Saxon times to Elizabethan times was an epoch of growth in England. A winter of decay followed. Then by mid-Eighteenth Century came the beginnings of a new spring, manifested in Britain in the field of mechanics and industry.

The Eighteenth Century, which marked an epoch of new beginnings, also marked an end of old institutions. To the French Revolution he gives his now usual interpretation, as the political event of the century and even of the era.

The French Revolution is seen, or begins everywhere to be seen, ' as the crowning phenomenon of our Modern Time '; ' the inevitable stern end of much; the fearful, but also wonderful, indispensable and sternly beneficent beginning of much.' . . . [It was] the most convulsive phenomenon of the last thousand years. Europe lay pining, obstructed, moribund, quack-ridden, hag-ridden. . . .[62]

[61] *Ibid.*, IV, 181.   [62] *Ibid.*, IV, 150.

The world was then united in " sorrowfulest *dis*belief that there is properly speaking any truth in the world." The faith of men, he says, was then dead; and spiritual life had departed.[63] It was that era of disbelief that the French Revolution ended.

But on the constructive side, the French Revolution did nothing; for democracy is merely transitional. Though democracy is advancing fast,

all men may see, whose sight is good for much, that in democracy can lie no finality; that with the completest winning of democracy there is nothing yet won,—except emptiness, and the free chance to win! Democracy is, by the nature of it, a self-cancelling business; and gives in the long-run a net result of *zero*. Where no government is wanted, save that of the parish-constable, as in America with its boundless soil, every man being able to find work and recompense for himself, democracy may subsist; not elsewhere, except briefly, as a swift transition towards something other and farther.[64] . . . Democracy, take it where you will in our Europe, is found but as a regulated method of rebellion and abrogation; it abrogates the old arrangement of things; and leaves . . . *zero* and vacuity for the institution of a new arrangement.[65]

Later he adds his own social panacea. It is grounded on the recognition that " a man *has* his superiors, a regular hierarchy above him; extending up . . . to Heaven itself. . . ." [66] And for man's social and political happiness, he prescribes not the equality of a democracy, but the inequalities of a hierarchy of superiors.

Though in *Chartism* Carlyle discusses past history by reference to a scheme of alternating epochs, considers the French Revolution as the end of an epoch of disbelief, denounces democracy as rebellion or at best

[63] *Ibid.*, IV, 151
[64] *Ibid.*, IV, 158.

[65] *Ibid.*, IV, 159.
[66] *Ibid.*, IV, 189.

emptiness, and insists on government by a hierarchy of superiors, he nevertheless comments adversely upon Saint-Simonism. Bewailing the break in continuity in the old priesthood of France, he exclaims:

That one whole generation of thinkers should be without a religion to believe, or even to contradict; that Christianity, in thinking France, should as it were fade away so long into a remote extraneous tradition, was one of the saddest facts connected with the future of that country. Look at such Political and Moral Philosophies, St.-Simonisms, Robert-Macairisms, and the 'Literature of Desperation'! Kingship was perhaps but a cheap waste, compared with this of the Priestship; under which France still, all but unconsciously, labours; and may long labour, remediless the while.[67]

The context of that comment on the Saint-Simonians should be noted. It shows that Carlyle is again denouncing the Saint-Simonian religion, or at most the Saint-Simonian polity insofar as it had set up religious pretenses and had attempted to replace the older, super-natural religion.[68]

The final exhibit of evidence in this chapter is *Heroes and Hero-Worship*. These lectures of 1840 are, in their published form of 1841, perhaps the best-known book that Carlyle wrote. As Mrs. Young points out, that fact is ironical; for the popularity of these lectures perhaps leads to a misinterpretation of Carlyle's basic concept of history. The misinterpretation lies in the over-stress on individualism and the consequent under-stress on the

---

[67] *Ibid.*, IV, 161.

[68] And those grounds for the denunciation should be kept in mind. Otherwise the reader will be confused when, in the decade about to open, he finds Carlyle repeatedly advocating social views that he had learned from the Saint-Simonians and that he had developed on the broad basis of the Saint-Simonian philosophy of history. The details of the social philosophy, in their connection with the philosophy of history, will be treated in a later study.

historical process of which the individual is a part.[69] Mrs. Young's observation is pertinent to the present study; for, although the Saint-Simonian concept of great men may have had some influence on Carlyle's Hero, our present interest is Carlyle's concept of the process, or law, of history. Doubtless many influences went into the shaping of his concept of historical periodicity as it is expressed in the Hero lectures.[70] For example, Fichte's *Über das Wesen des Gelehrten*, the Norse myth of the Twilight of the Gods, and Goethe's "Israel in der Wüste," to mention only three obvious ones, influenced both the content and the form of Carlyle's expression of the concept. But the presence of such important elements must not be allowed to obscure the fact that the basic law of progressive periodic mutation and the application of that law in *Heroes* bear a striking resemblance to the Saint-Simonian influence that we have been tracing. This is far and away the most important influence on *Heroes* so far as a great many details of Carlyle's view of the historical process are concerned, so far as those details are articulated into a concept of historical periodicity, and so far as actual history is interpreted in conformity with that concept. All of those influences—as Carlyle uses them—[71] are harmonious with, and fit into, the Saint-Simonian concept.

Early in the Hero lectures, much of Carlyle's concept of periodicity is expressed in a passage on mutation and

[69] Louise Merwin Young, *Thomas Carlyle and the Art of History*, pp. 81-86.
[70] Professor B. H. Lehman's study, *Carlyle's Theory of the Hero: Its Sources, Development, History, and Influence on Carlyle's Work. A Study of a Nineteenth Century Idea* (Durham, Duke University Press, 1928), excellently illustrates the variety of influences on *Heroes*.
[71] Carlyle's adaptation of Fichte distorts Fichte's meaning. See *ante*, pp. 104-105, note 100.

progress. The context deals with the Norse myth of The Twilight of the Gods.

Curious: this law of mutation, which also is a law written in man's inmost thought . . . ; though all dies, and even gods die, yet all death is but a phoenix fire-death, and new-birth into the Greater and the Better! It is the fundamental Law of Being for a creature made of Time, living in this Place of Hope.[72]

And later he comments thus on the modern concept of Progress of the Species:

. . . the fact itself [of progress] seems certain enough; nay we can trace-out the inevitable necessity of it in the nature of things. . . . It is the history of every man; and in the history of Mankind we see it summed-up into great historical amounts,—revolutions, new epochs.[73]

It is noteworthy that the last sentence just quoted specifies the sociological, *a posteriori*, method of proving progress—rather than Fichte's psychological, or logical *a priori*, method. So much for Carlyle's statement, in 1840-1841, of the law of progressive change.

His characterization of the alternate epochs by which that law of progress functions is an illuminating example of his simultaneous use of the Saint-Simonians and Goethe. Immersed in the welter of things, thoughtful man (Carlyle explains) may long for some interpretation, some theory of the universe that he can believe. And

Thought once awakened does not again slumber; unfolds itself into a System of Thought; grows, in man after man, generation after generation,—till its full stature is reached, and *such* System of Thought can grow no further, but must give place to another.[74]

[72] *On Heroes, Hero-Worship and the Heroic in History*, p. 39.
[73] *Ibid.*, p. 118.   [74] *Ibid.*, pp. 21-22.

As long as the schema, or theory of the universe, remains credible, he adds, the age continues fruitful. For life is then united by a directive principle.

Belief is great, life-giving. The history of a Nation becomes fruitful, soul-elevating, great, so soon as it believes.[75] . . . The believing man is the original man. . . . Whole ages, what we call ages of Faith, are original; all men in them, or most of the men in them, sincere. These are the great and fruitful ages. . . . There is true union, true kingship, loyalty. . . .[76]

However, no matter how excellent the schema, or directive principle, may be, it must be only approximate; it therefore in the course of time becomes inadequate and incredible.

It is notable enough, surely, how a Theorem or Spiritual Representation, so we may call it, which once took-in the whole Universe, and was completely satisfactory in all parts of it to the highly-discursive acute intellect of Dante, one of the greatest in the world,—had in the course of another century become dubitable to common intellects. . . . Why could not Dante's Catholicism continue; but Luther's Protestantism must needs follow? Alas, nothing will *continue*.[77]

Here again, after a decade, is the old familiar juice of *Sartor*, and even more notably, of " Characteristics."

The method of transition between an old period and a new period Carlyle again represents by the phoenix figure. A striking passage on the phoenix has already been quoted: ". . . though all dies, and even gods die, yet all death is but a phoenix fire-death, and new-birth into the Greater and the Better! " [78] This phoenix-doctrine of transition is implicit in the whole discussion

---

[75] *Ibid.*, p. 77.
[76] *Ibid.*, p. 126. Page 172, he says: ". . . the battle of Belief against Unbelief is the never-ending battle! "
[77] *Ibid.*, pp. 117-118.   [78] *Ibid.*, p. 39.

of the historic process in *Heroes*. It will be especially notable in Carlyle's later comments, in the same book, on Protestantism, which replaced Catholicism, and on the French Revolution and democracy, which displaced feudalism.

In designating the periods in actual past history, *Heroes* has nothing to say about the period in which the directive principle was classical pagan polytheism. Two years before, in the lectures on European literature, Carlyle had dealt with that period, and had dealt with it in almost exactly the Saint-Simonian way. But in the 1840 lectures he works this side the classics. He does not even make his customary comparison between the French Revolution and the Northern Invasions. But on the second great period he has a considerable number of important comments. Some of the most important for our purposes show the similarity between him and the Saint-Simonians in treating the two directive principles of the period: Catholic religion and feudal polity.

The Christian Faith, which was the theme of Dante's Song, had produced this Practical Life which Shakspeare was to sing.[79] . . . Dante has given us the Faith or soul; Shakspeare, in a not less noble way, has given us the Practice or body.[80]

[79] *Ibid.*, p. 102. In spite of the Protestantism of Professor Dover Wilson's Hamlet, one recalls Heine's statement that Shakespeare was a continuator and interpreter of Catholicism. It is perhaps unnecessary to point out here that Heine was associated with the Saint-Simonians and to suggest that his statement and Carlyle's may have a common background in the Saint-Simonian philosophy of history. Such suggestions verge over into aesthetics, which we must leave for a future discussion.

[80] *Ibid.*, p. 101. In this connection, it is interesting to compare (1) Carlyle's distinction here between two romantics, in order to harmonize his aesthetics with the Saint-Simonian philosophy of history, and (2) Coleridge's distinction (*Lectures*, Everyman edition, p. 26) between classics and romantics, in order to harmonize his aesthetic with the Kantian psychology.

And Carlyle adds that Shakespeare appeared just when chivalry had reached its last polish and was on the point of breaking down. " Dante's sublime Catholicism . . . has to be torn asunder by a Luther; Shakspeare's noble Feudalism . . . has to end in a French Revolution." [81] In *Heroes,* he finds a way to work the English Puritan, or Civil Wars, era into the Saint-Simonian framework of history.

Protestantism . . . is the work of a Prophet: the prophet-work of that sixteenth century. The first stroke of honest demolition to an ancient thing grown false and idolatrous; preparatory afar off to a new thing, which shall be true, and authentically divine! . . . Protestantism was a revolt against spiritual sovereignties, Popes and much else. Nay I will grant that English Puritanism, revolt against earthly sovereignties, was the second act of it; that the enormous French Revolution itself was the third act, whereby all sovereignties earthly and spiritual were, as might seem, abolished or made sure of abolition. Protestantism is the grand root from which our whole subsequent European History branches out.[82]

If that emphasis on Puritanism is the reflection of Carlyle's growing interest in England's national past and in Cromwell, it nevertheless fits well into the Saint-Simonian scheme of history. And he continues to consider the French Revolution the culmination of Eighteenth Century scepticism; it is the great event that swept clean the way for a better future order that it and its generation could not develop.

Scepticism, for that [Eighteenth] century, we must consider as the decay of the old ways of believing, the preparation afar off for new better and wider ways,—an inevitable

---

[81] *On Heroes,* p. 119.

[82] *Ibid.,* p. 123. A practically identical passage on The Three Acts occurs on p. 237. And the dramatic figure of speech is carried further, with changed implications, in Carlyle's last great work, *Frederick.*

thing. We will not blame men for it; we will lament their hard fate. We will understand that destruction of old *forms* is not destruction of everlasting *substances*; that Scepticism, as sorrowful and hateful as we see it, is not an end but a beginning.[83]

Napoleon, understanding the destructive aspect of the French Revolution along with the anarchic aspect of the democracy which it produced, at first attempted to provide an organizing principle:

To bridle-in that great devouring, self-devouring French Revolution; to *tame* it, so that it may become *organic*, and be able to live among other organisms and *formed* things, not as a wasting destruction alone: is not this still what he partly aimed at . . . ?[84] And did he not interpret the dim purport of it [The French Revolution and Democracy] well? '*La carrière ouverte aux talens,* The implements to him who can handle them ': this actually is the truth, and even the whole truth; it includes whatever the French Revolution, or any Revolution, could mean.[85]

Finally, we must at least glance at the prophet. For by 1840 Carlyle was rapidly assuming the mantle, to denounce democracy as inevitable but empty.

All this [talk and confusion] of Liberty and Equality, Electoral suffrages, Independence and so forth, we will take . . . to be a temporary phenomenon, by no means a final one. Though likely to last a long time, with sad enough embroilments for us all, we must welcome it, as the penalty of sins that are past, the pledge of inestimable benefits that are coming. In all ways, it behoved men to quit simulacra and return to fact; cost what it might, that did behove to be done. . . . You cannot make an association out of insincere men. . . . In all this wild revolutionary work, from Protestantism downwards, I see the blessedest result preparing

[83] *Ibid.,* p. 172.   [84] *Ibid.,* p. 240.
[85] *Ibid.,* pp. 239-240. Compare this interpretation of Napoleon with the Saint-Simonian interpretation. See *supra,* ch. II, p. 44, note 29 (next to last ¶).

itself: not abolition of Hero-worship, but rather what I would call a whole World of Heroes. . . . A world all sincere, a believing world: the like has been; the like will again be,—cannot help being.[86]

Again and again, now and in the next decade, he is to urge belief, sincerity, and hero-worship as the panacea for a sick World, sick Europe, sick England.

It seems to me, you lay your finger here on the heart of the world's maladies, when you call it a Sceptical World. An insincere world; a godless untruth of a world! It is out of this . . . that the whole tribe of social pestilences, French Revolutions, Chartisms, and what not, have derived their being,—their chief necessity to be. This must alter.[87]

Then will come union, organization spiritual and material, about an organizing principle that is adequate and credible; and it will be nobler than Catholicism and feudalism.[88] The organizing motif—if not the principle—will be hero-worship; and the government will be " a *Hero*-archy . . . or a Hierarchy," based upon " reverence and obedience done to men really great and wise." [89]

Though *Heroes* contains no specific reference to the Saint-Simonians and though it does not present a connected discussion of the whole span of European culture, it does contain a good many passages of importance to our discussion. The list of significant items indicated in those passages is worth recalling: the basic law of progress through periodic mutation; the characterization of alternate epochs; the description of the way in which the various schemata, or theories of the universe,

---

[86] *Ibid.*, p. 127. Again, p. 12, he denounces democracy, liberty, and equality as false bank-notes.

[87] *Ibid.*, p. 175. The rest of this passage closely resembles the last part of the passage just quoted.

[88] *Ibid.*, p. 136.   [89] *Ibid.*, p. 12.

develop and then become incredible and obsolete; the method of transition between the historical periods that are unified by those various schemata; the tracing of the second great period in actual European history; the designation of the two organizing principles in religion and polity during that period; the contrast of those principles to the Protestant Reformation and the French Revolution; the interpretation of the French Revolution as the end of that period; the attitude toward the ensuing democracy; and the notion that the future organization of society will be hierarchic. These various items, each in some degree, and, especially, all of them together, as they articulate in a concept of historic process, suggest the influence of the Saint-Simonians.

This period of six years, 1835 to 1841, early in which Carlyle wrote his first great history, is, like the preceding period, highly important in the study of his use of the Saint-Simonian concept of historical periodicity. All the features except part of one element in the Saint-Simonian concept are repeatedly found in the work of these six years. And even that one part occurs about the middle of the period. In the first of the productions, *The French Revolution,* Carlyle insists on the law of progressive periodic mutation; he divides periods into alternate epochs of growth and disintegration in which various directive principles or schemata develop and then decay; and he stresses the phoenix method of transition between periods. Although his characterization of epochs is as usual closer to Goethe in wording than it is to the Saint-Simonians, his designation of the epochs in actual past history is closer to the Saint-Simonians. However, he does not reproduce the historical sketch that occurs in either of those sources. That is, he omits the whole of Goethe's Hebrew period.

And he omits the organic, or faithful, part of the Saint-Simonian pagan period. Furthermore, he actually departs from the Saint-Simonian sketch, when in one short passage he attempts to point out four subordinate positive epochs of merely national faiths, from the Fifteenth Century to the Eighteenth Century. But in his treatment of the medieval positive epoch he is again Saint-Simonian. Saint-Simonian also, as far as it goes, is his treatment of both of the decadent epochs. He alludes, though only briefly, to the Roman decadence; he puts much stress on the decadence that culminated in the Eighteenth Century. And his general interpretation of the French Revolution and of the resultant democracy is like the Saint-Simonian view. The two essays that may be considered by-products of *The French Revolution* both originally contained, it seems, derogatory comments on the religious aspects of Saint-Simonism. Nevertheless the interpretation of the French Revolution in the second essay is the Saint-Simonian interpretation. Almost immediately after the completion of *The French Revolution,* Carlyle began his series of annual lectures, two sets of which have survived. The first of the surviving sets—*Lectures on the History of Literature,* 1838—contains some impressive evidence. These *Lectures,* though lacking Carlyle's increasingly common statements concerning the political and social organization of the future, contain the other four Saint-Simonian elements in a completeness found nowhere else in Carlyle's works. That is, the *Lectures* contain the statement of the law of progressive periodic mutation, the characterization of alternating epochs of belief and unbelief (correctly ascribed by Carlyle to Goethe, but perfectly fused with the larger Saint-Simonian concept), the phoenix doctrine of transition between periods, and—an element not found complete elsewhere in Carlyle—the designation and tracing of all four of the epochs in two full historical periods. In this last element, the very close detailed similarities between Carlyle and the Saint-Simonians in sketching the last 2300 years of European history, from pre-Socratic Greece to Revolutionary France, should complete the conviction of anyone who has doubted until he has seen all five of the Saint-Simonian elements reproduced. It is true that *Chartism,* 1839, contains a disparaging allusion to the religious pretensions of the Saint-Simonian polity and that it lacks the explicitness of the *Lectures* of 1838 in presenting many of the elements of the Saint-Simonian concept of historical periodicity. However, it does imply the concept, for it discusses medieval and modern European history by reference to periodical alternation of epochs. Furthermore, *Chartism* supplies the element lacking in the *Lectures on the History of Literature*—the interpretation of present and future society in harmony with the Saint-Simonian concept of periodicity. In the last series of the annual lectures, *Heroes,* he again insists on the law of progressive periodic mutation and specifies the sociological method of proving it; describes the way in which various schemata, or theories of the universe, develop in the unified epochs and then become incredible and obsolete in alternate epochs; stresses the phoenix transition between periods; designates and traces the second great period of European history with its two organizing principles, or schemata; interprets the French Revolution and modern democracy in the Saint-Simonian way; and points to a hierarchic organization of future society.

Throughout the period of Carlyle's writing now under

discussion, the outspokenness and assurance of Carlyle's comments on current social matters increases steadily.[90] And now, as his greatest decade of social prophecy begins, we must accustom ourselves to stopping short, time and again, with a mere cursory glance at his analysis of present social ills and at the remedies that he proposed. With his growing stress on the present and future condition of England, his expositions of the whole

[90] It is interesting to note how early, in times of great intellectual change, Carlyle became aware of the process that was going on in his mind. For example, on April 13, 1839 (some months before *Chartism*), he wrote Emerson: ". . . I wait in silence for the new chapter, feeling truly that we are at the end of one period here. I count it *two* in my autobiography: we shall see what the *third* is; [if] third there be. But I am in small haste for a third." *Correspondence of Carlyle and Emerson,* I, 231). Indeed, students of Carlyle's life can identify each of the three periods here alluded to. The first period to which Carlyle refers was the period in which he worked out his individual philosophy of life, as can be seen in his primarily literary productions. The second period, which falls within the limits of the present study and which we have therefore already shown him heralding in March 1830 (see *ante,* p. 7), is the one in which he worked out his philosophy of history. The third period, of which he announced the approach in 1839, is the one in which he worked out his social philosophy. The present chapter of our study has shown the pertinent parts of his philosophy of history; the next chapter will at least reflect (though it cannot show in detail) his new stress on social interests.

The organic nature of the transition that led up to those periods is worth a further comment here. In each transition, there was gradual shift of emphasis, rather than sudden change of continuity; for the changes we have in mind were primarily intellectual rather than emotional in character. Not only did the various periods arrive at their full fruits (such as *Sartor, The French Revolution,* and *Past and Present,* respectively) years after the changes first became noticeable; but also the full fruits of each period show beautifully the effects of all the preceding intellectual developments through which Carlyle had gone. Emotional attendants, in each case, there were—fearful attendants sometimes—in Carlyle, of all men. But here we dare not digress into the strong inward compunctions that came on Leith Walk, or into the little unremembered acts at Hoddam Hill, Craigenputtock, and Cheyne Row. They are among the materials of biography. We are studying a limited phase of the history of an idea.

process of history come to be fore-shortened. And, especially important, in view of that fact, is the completeness of his exposition of all the features of the Saint-Simonian concept of historical periodicity in the writings that he produced within the period from 1835 to 1841. There are reasons, as we have seen and as we shall see, to believe that a leading clue to his analysis of social ills, as well as to some of the remedies that he proposed, was the concept of historical periodicity that he had found in the Saint-Simonian writings, that he had fused harmoniously with otherwise-derived elements, and that he had used in all of its features—most of them repeatedly—by 1841.

CHAPTER VI

LATTER DAYS, FROM *Past and Present* (1843) ON

There is danger that this last chapter, slender as it is in evidence of Saint-Simonian influence on Carlyle's philosophy of history, will leave a false impression. But such a danger attends any partial study. Actually one phase, which we cannot here discuss, of Saint-Simonian influence remained strong and even increased. If this study had centered upon the influence of the Saint-Simonians on Carlyle's social analysis, the chapter including *Past and Present* and *Latter-Day Pamphlets* would show the climax in detailed resemblances. One scholar,[1] who has perhaps not exhausted the evidence, finds reasons that culminate in *Past and Present* to call Carlyle a disciple of Saint-Simon. But Carlyle's social debt to the Saint-Simonians cannot be properly estimated without understanding the philosophy of history on which his social philosophy rests. And it is the task of the present final chapter to carry through the examination of the philosophy of history that, though frequently suggested or implied in Carlyle's latter writings, runs under the surface of them, vitalizing and unifying the social thought.

The only specific allusion to the Saint-Simonians that I have found during the decade of the 1840's occurs in 1843, in *Past and Present*. Like the references late in the preceding decade, it is a denunciation of their religious pretensions.

---

[1] Professor Cofer, whose work has been characterized earlier in this study (see *ante,* p. viii and note 7).

156

. . . O Advanced-Liberal, one cannot promise thee any ' New Religion,' for some time. . . . . . . I will as soon think of making Galaxies and Star-Systems to guide little herring-vessels by, as of preaching Religion that the Constable may continue possible. O my Advanced-Liberal friend, this new second progress, of proceeding ' to invent God,' is a very strange one! Jacobinism unfolded into Saint-Simonism bodes innumerable blessed things; but the thing itself might draw tears from a Stoic! [2]

Though many passages in *Past and Present* show similarity to the Saint-Simonian social philosophy, only a few reflect the Saint-Simonian philosophy of history. There is no specific statement of the law of progressive periodic mutation, no characterization of epochs of faith and epochs of unfaith, and no discussion of the phoenix, or palingenetic, method of transition between periods. But resemblances occur in the designation of one past epoch as organic and in the prophecy of a future organic epoch, in the belief that a completely new society must replace the old, in the interpretation of the French Revolution as the end of the old period, and in several denunciations of the present democratic tendencies as inadequate.

Those few points will be presented briefly in the order just named. The organic epochs past and future are both of them suggestive of the Saint-Simonians, even in terminology:

We will now quit this of the hard, organic, but limited Feudal Ages; and glance timidly into the immense Industrial Ages, as yet all inorganic, and in a quite pulpy condition, requiring desperately to harden themselves into some organism! [3]

And elsewhere too he calls attention to the need of a

[2] *Past and Present* (London, Chapman and Hall, 1897) pp. 225-226.
[3] *Ibid.*, p. 249.

complete social change: " A total change of regimen, change of constitution and existence from the very centre of it; a new body to be got, with resuscitated soul. . . ." [4] He indicates two significant phenomena of the change, one of which is the French Revolution.

A French Revolution is one phenomenon; as complement and spiritual exponent thereof, a poet Goethe and German literature is to me another. The old Secular or Practical World, so to speak, having gone up in fire, is not here the prophecy and dawn of a new Spiritual World, parent of far nobler, wider, new Practical Worlds? [5]

However, the new world is not to be a democracy. Several times he denounces, as did the Saint-Simonians, the current ballot-boxes, equality, liberty, and independence. For they all seemed to him negative, inadequate for a new era. [6] On the whole, the concept of history in *Past and Present* shows few signs of Saint-Simonian influence: mentions of the past organic feudal age and future organic industrial age, comments on the necessity of a complete social change, interpretation of the French Revolution as the end of a period, and denunciations of liberalism.

Again, in *Cromwell* (1845) Carlyle does not attempt to discuss the whole theory of history. His stress is of course primarily on the Seventeenth Century and on dramatizing the events of that era. He does not even state the law of progressive periodic mutation as a law. Perhaps periodicity is implied. But it is only implied, not expressed. One passage begins by saying that the action of the Regicides struck a blow to the heart of flunkeyism; and from that blow, he adds, flunkeyism and cant have ever since been sick and now are dying. And the sentences that immediately succeed those

[4] *Ibid.*, p. 36.   [5] *Ibid.*, p. 236.   [6] *Ibid.*, pp. 83, 168, 287.

statements perhaps imply the periodic recurrence of epochs of belief followed by epochs of cant and following them.

The like of which [Regicide] action will not be needed for a thousand years again. Needed, alas—not till a new genuine Hero-worship has arisen, has perfected itself; and had time to degenerate into a Flunkyism and Cloth-worship again![7]

In that comment, which is not a statement of law as general law, he does not specifically say that genuine hero-worshipping ages are temporary because their schemata are only approximately true. But in a later volume of the same work, he probably has in mind that general law when he makes the following special application: "—Why Puritanism could not continue? My friend, Puritanism was *not* the Complete Theory of this immense Universe; no, only a part thereof! "[8]

Anyone who can see the implication of a law of periodic mutation in the passage just presented will have no trouble tracing in the following passage a reminiscence of Goethe's general characterization of the epochs of unfaith.

Considerable tracts of Ages there have been, by far the majority indeed, wherein the men . . . were a set of mimetic creatures rather than men; without heart-insight as to this Universe . . . ; without conviction or belief of their own regarding it, at all;—who walked merely by hear-says. . . . These are the Unheroic Ages; which cannot serve . . . except as *dust,* as inorganic manure. The memory of such Ages fades away for ever out of the minds of all men. . . .

Good reader, if you be wise, search not for the secret of Heroic Ages . . . among their falsities. . . . . . . the Age was Heroic even because it had declared war to the death with these. . . .[9]

[7] *Oliver Cromwell's Letters and Speeches, with Elucidations,* I, 414.
[8] *Ibid.,* IV, 184.   [9] *Ibid.,* I, 83-84.

Of the suggestive passages in *Cromwell,* the passage just given comes the nearest to being a general characterization of what Goethe called epochs of faith and what the Saint-Simonians called essentially religious organic epochs.

The third element for which we are accustomed to look—the phoenix-like, or palingenetic, transition between historical periods—is not discussed in *Cromwell.*

The tracing of the various periods and epochs in past history is far from full or elaborate. Nothing is said about the classical period. And of what the Saint-Simonians called the organic epoch of the second period occurs only this brief reminiscence:

For many centuries, Catholic Christianity, a fit embodiment of that divine Sense [of difference between right and wrong], had been current more or less, making the generations noble: and here in England, in the Century called the Seventeenth, we see the last aspect of it hitherto,—not the last of all, it is to be hoped.[10]

Thus much of the great Catholic directive principle, schema, theory of the universe! By the Seventeenth Century, according to Carlyle's *Cromwell,* adherence to that once great theory had become mere cant. And the Seventeenth Century Puritan theory of the universe had become the *sine qua non.* From the standpoint of English history, Carlyle was nearer correct in designating the Seventeenth Century as the end of Catholicism, than he would have been if he had followed the continental Saint-Simonians' designation of Luther's century as the end. Certainly Carlyle's nationalism had undergone great development during the preceding decade. Now, as in the lectures of 1838, he almost con-

[10] *Ibid.,* I, 51.

siders Puritanism one of the great fruitful epochs of faith, of which Goethe had generalized. The Second Civil War, Carlyle says, ended " in abolition of Cobwebs;—if it be possible, in a Government of Heroism and Veracity; at lowest, of Anti-Flunkyism, Anti-Cant, and the *endeavour* after Heroism and Veracity." [11] Puritanism was " A practical world based on Belief in God;—such as many centuries had seen before, but as never any century since has been privileged to see." [12] In that nationalistic stressing of Seventeenth Century English Puritanism, instead of tracing the various periods and epochs in European history, there is little that suggests the Saint-Simonian influence.

In Carlyle's fore-glimpse of the future he says that, if England is to struggle Godward again, it will have to do so from the foundation of sincere belief that Cromwell laid. For after its two centuries of cant, England now finds itself choking. [13]

If it please Heaven, these Two-hundred Years of universal Cant in speech, with so much of Cotton-spinning, Coalboring, Commercing, and other valuable Sincerity of Work, going-on the while, shall not be quite lost to us! Our Cant will vanish. . . . We shall awaken; and find ourselves in a world greatly *widened*. [14]

If the examination of *Cromwell* shows anything of the Saint-Simonian concept of history, it does so by implication. The law of periodic mutation is implied, along with its corollary that no theory of the universe can be permanent. The Goethean characterization of epochs of belief and unbelief is more nearly echoed. But

[11] *Ibid.*, I, 414.
[12] *Ibid.*, I, 81. Several other passages stress religious faith as the leading characteristic of Puritanism: e. g., I, 4, and 82.
[13] *Ibid.*, III, 2; IV, 207-208.   [14] *Ibid.*, IV, 184.

there is no discussion of the phoenix-doctrine of transition between periods. And there is no tracing-out of the periods that the Saint-Simonians traced in past history. Instead, there is nearly exclusive stress upon Puritanism; the Puritan era is exalted almost into the role of an epoch of faith; and England is prophetically warned to return to the faith of the Pilgrim Fathers.

A striking result in 1848 of Carlyle's social speculations was his unpublished manuscript entitled " Industrial Regiments." One brief passage written about the middle of November suggests in idea and in diction a connection with the concept of historical periodicity. Carlyle's alludes thus to the condition of society in the middle of the Seventeenth Century:

in short a coherent system of society, that was organic, that could and did cohere, bound together by the authentic wants and beliefs of men, and resting on the eternal foundation of things.[14a]

But, however well the passage conforms to the Saint-Simonian characterizations of organic epochs, it fails to correspond to the chronology of any organic epoch designated by the Saint-Simonians.

With the events of 1848 in Europe, Carlyle became even more of the prophet speaking in the language of prophecy. In December he wrote to his frined Varnhagen von Ense about the career of sansculottism since the preceding February. To Carlyle it seemed in itself a terrible thing. But, from his interpretation of the course of history, it seemed the fulfillment of an eternal prophecy, a general bankruptcy of falsity, and " der

---

[14a] The unpublished manuscript " Industrial Regiments " is now in the Manuscript Vault of Yale University Library. The passage just quoted occurs on the unnumbered side of the ninth sheet.

Beginn einer Neugeburt der Welt." [15]   And less than two years later, in *Latter-Day Pamphlets*, he attempted to thrust the same interpretation before England.

The *Latter-Day Pamphlets* (1850) lack much of the general theorizing about the course of history that Carlyle had used in the decade of the 1830's. However, although the *Pamphlets* were primarily a series of strident warnings to his own times, much of his earlier thought about world-history does at least show through those pieces. Perhaps the most pertinent evidence of his belief in a law of progressive mutation is his statement,

. . . I see . . . the world ripening towards glorious new developments, unimagined hitherto,—of which this abominable mud deluge itself [Jesuitism, falsity], threatening to submerge us all, was the inevitable precursor, and the means decreed by the Eternal.[16]

Obviously in the latter words of that sentence he is expressing his meaning in terms of religious prophecy instead of terms of historical law. Indeed the sentence is far from a statement of any law, though it does recognize the existence of a law of progressive mutation. Later evidence, as we shall see, suggests that the mutation is periodic.

Nowhere in the *Pamphlets* does he say that each period is divided into alternate epochs of faith and unfaith. But to one who has examined Carlyle's earlier utterances from 1831 to 1841 on that point, the following passage reflects Goethe's notion that epochs of noble activity are characterized by faith in directive prin-

[15] *Briefe Thomas Carlyle's an Varnhagen von Ense aus den Jahren 1837-1857* (Uebersetzt und herausgegeben von Richard Preuss, Berlin, Paetel, 1892), p. 112 (December 29, 1848).
[16] *Latter-Day Pamphlets* (London, Chapman and Hall, 1898), "Jesuitism," p. 329 (August 1, 1850).

ciples, or schemata, and that epochs lacking such unifying faith are ignorable.

You say, The old ages had a noble belief about the world, and *therefore* were capable of a noble activity in the world. My friends, it is partly true: your Scepticism and Jesuitism, your ignoble no-belief, except what belief a beaver or judicious pig were capable of, is too undeniable. . . .[17]

Though neither palingenesia nor the phoenix-doctrine of transition between periods is stated as general law, and though those specific terms are not used, Carlyle does comment thus on one transition: " These days of universal death must be days of universal newbirth, if the ruin is not to be total and final! "[18] The death-birth notion here suggests the phoenix, and the word *newbirth* recalls *palingenesia*.

With respect to the various periods, and the alternate epochs within the periods, *Latter-Day Pamphlets* contains more on classicism than one would expect. Carlyle's contrast between the heroic age and the unheroic age in the classical period suggests the Saint-Simonian contrast between organic and critical epochs. The dichotomy of Greek and Roman classicism recalls the Saint-Simonian treatment and recalls too Carlyle's treatment of it in the lectures of 1838. And the inclusion of the Hebrew heroic phase reminds us again of Goethe. The suggestive, but far from elaborate, passage runs as follows:

Old Suetonius Romans, corrupt babbling Greeks of the Lower Empire, examples more than one: consider them; be taught by them, add not to the number of them. Heroism, not the apery and traditions of Heroism . . . : without this

---

[17] *Ibid.*, p. 333.
[18] *Ibid.*, " The Present Time," p. 2 (February 1, 1850).

there had been no Rome either; it was this that had made old Rome, old Greece, and old Judea.[19]

Concerning what the Saint-Simonians called the organic phase of Catholicism and feudalism, Carlyle is brief. Indeed he says nothing of feudalism, but centers his comment on Catholic Jesuitism. Ignatius, or the once vital Jesuitism, he says, is now fast sinking to the abyss,

dragging much along with him thither. Whole worlds along with him: such continents of things, once living and beautiful, now dead and horrible; things once sacred, now not even commonly profane. . . .[20]

The decadent phase of the once vital principle of the Middle Ages has considerably more treatment in *Latter-Day Pamphlets*. After a glance at Luther, Carlyle proceeds toward the final stage of the destruction: i. e., the French Revolution.

. . . Luther and Protestantism Proper having, so to speak, withdrawn from the battlefield, as entities whose work was done, there then appeared on it Jean Jacques and French Sansculottism; to which all creatures have gradually joined themselves. Whereby now we have Protestantism *Im-* proper,—a Protestantism universal and illimitable on the part of all men; the whole world risen into anarchic mutiny, with pike and paving-stone; swearing . . . that Ignatius and Imposture shall not rule them any more . . . ; but that they will go unruled rather. . . .[21]

He repeatedly says that England for the last two centuries—and Europe still longer—has lain in a death-

---

[19] *Ibid.*, " Jesuitism," p. 331 (August 1, 1850). And again, as frequently in the works before this time, Carlyle compared modern anarchy—this time of 1848—to the destruction of the Roman Empire by the Northern Barbarians. See *ibid.*, " The Present Time," p. 6 (February 1, 1850).

[20] *Ibid.*, " Jesuitism," p. 307 (August 1, 1850).

[21] *Ibid.*, pp. 306-307.

like sleep of falsity and hypocrisy.[22] Only since 1789 has man been awakening out of that torpor "into the Sorcerer's Sabbath of Anarchy." [23] And that latter condition, anarchy or democracy, is important only because it is a necessary stage in man's progress toward a better order.[24] The degree of completeness with which Carlyle in these social pamphlets runs up the scale of European history as far as to latter-day democracy, from classical times to Victorian times, is perhaps surprising. But the significance of his statements is, for our present purpose, very elusive. In the following points, Carlyle is tantalizingly like the Saint-Simonians: in his mere glance at the two phases of classicism, apparently preserving within those phases the dichotomy of Grecian and Roman; in his brief statement about the vital phase of Catholicism; in his more elaborate comment on the later decadent phase up to the French Revolution; and in his recognition of the French Revolution as the destroyer of the old at the same time that it is the preparer for the new.

As had been his custom for years, in regarding the French Revolution as the bringer-in of anarchy or democracy, Carlyle equates democracy and anarchy. And while denouncing them as inadequate for the future era, he blesses them as necessary preparers of the way for the new era. This attitude toward democracy is, at least in part, the product of the concept of progressive periodic mutation.

Democracy . . . is here:—for sixty years now, ever since the grand or *First* French Revolution, that fact has been terribly announced to all the world. . . .

[22] *Ibid.*, "Hudson's Statue," p. 278 (July 1, 1850), and "Jesuitism," pp. 293 and 312 (August 1, 1850).
[23] *Ibid.*, "Jesuitism," p. 312 (August 1, 1850).
[24] *Ibid.*, p. 312, and "The Present Time," p. 22 (February 1, 1850).

What *is* Democracy; this huge inevitable Product of the Destinies, which is everywhere the portion of our Europe in these latter days? There lies the question for us.[25]

Historically speaking, I believe there was no Nation that could subsist upon Democracy.[26]

The same philosophy of history that had fostered such an attitude toward democracy had fostered Carlyle's deep faith that there would be, must be, a completely new social organization to replace by organic development the inadequate and now virtually non-existent one: " These days of universal death must be days of universal new-birth, if the ruin is not to be total and final! . . . A veritable ' New Era.'. . ."[27] The society in that new era, he believes, will have to be a monarchy, a hierarchy. For " The Universe itself is a Monarchy and Hierarchy. . . ."[28] There can be no equality: " The Noble in the high place, the Ignoble in the low; that is, in all times and in all countries, the Almighty Maker's Law."[29]

The incidental comments in *Latter-Day Pamphlets* on the historical process are hard to evaluate. The reason is that they are incidental. From them alone, without Carlyle's known earlier practice to furnish an hypothesis, an investigator would not induce the whole of the Saint-Simonian concept of the historical process. Nor would he be likely to induce any other equally inclusive concept of process. But hypothesis has a legitimate use. Accordingly, each one of the incidental comments has been held up for comparison with the comparable part of the Saint-Simonian formula of historical periodicity. Many of them fell far short of that formula; but they fell short, rather than differed. Apparently they fell short because in *Latter-Day*

[25] *Ibid.*, " The Present Time," p. 9 (February, 1, 1850).
[26] *Ibid.*, p. 18. [27] *Ibid.*, p. 2. [28] *Ibid.*, p. 21. [29] *Ibid.*, p. 22.

Pamphlets Carlyle was not trying to present an exposition of the whole of any historic process. He was primarily advocating British social reform rather than stating the background process that validated in his mind his diagnosis and his prescription. Insofar as his incidental comments on process have reference, they seem to be referable to, and to harmonize with, the Saint-Simonian concept that we have been tracing. That is, without here formulating a law of progressive periodic mutation, he recognizes the existence of the law. Without stating that progress proceeds through alternate epochs of faith and scepticism, he reflects Goethe's characterization of those epochs. Without stating any doctrine concerning transition between periods, Carlyle in pointing out one transition uses terminology that recalls his phoenix-doctrine and palingenesia. Without any apparent effort to trace-out the history of Europe, he touches lightly but suggestively several important points of the two historical periods that the Saint-Simonians identified in the European past. Like the Saint-Simonians, he considers the French Revolution as the end and destroyer of the old period and as the preparer for a new era. And he equates democracy with anarchy, considers democracy inadequate for the new era, and insists that the new social organization will be hierarchic instead of equalitarian.

What seems to be his last published comment on the Saint-Simonians occurs in the biography of John Sterling, written in 1851. The biography records how the mercurial Sterling had in 1828 made a quick trip to Paris,

and seen with no undue enthusiasm the Saint-Simonian Portent just beginning to preach for itself, and France in general simmering under a scum of impieties, levities, Saint-Simonisms, and frothy fantasticalities of all kinds, towards the boiling-over which soon made the Three Days of July famous.[30]

That statement seems to be only another of Carlyle's condemnations of the Saint-Simonians' fantastic religious sectarianism.[30a]

Frederick the Great, the last great work (1858-1865), does not provide even as much evidence as *Latter-Day Pamphlets* on the generalized law of progressive periodic mutation. The one general characterization of epochs sounds more like Fichte's characterization than it does like Goethe's or the Saint-Simonians'.[31] And general

---

[30] *The Life of John Sterling* (London, Chapman and Hall, 1897), p. 47. Probably after this time, as certainly before it, Carlyle discussed the Saint-Simonians in his conversations. There must have been considerable unrecorded talk in the 1830's between him and Mill on the subject. And after 1835 he may have discussed the subject with John Sterling, for in preparing his *Life of Sterling* he was able to give 1828 as the date of Sterling's interest in the Saint-Simonians. See Anne Kimball Tuell, " Carlyle's Marginalia in Sterling's *Essays and Tales,*" *P M L A,* LIV (September, 1939), 817.

[30a] This comment on the Saint-Simonians recalls Carlyle's hostile comments on Comte, the one-time disciple of Saint-Simon (see D. A. Wilson, *Carlyle at His Zenith, 1848-53* [London, 1927], p. 418 [July 1852]; Carlyle, *Essays,* V, 22 [1867]; and Froude, *Thomas Carlyle . . . 1834-1881,* II, 399 [June 8, 1868]). Enfantin too denounced Comte as a mechanizer of life and a destroyer of life (see *Oeuvres de Saint-Simon et d'Enfantin,* II, 65, note 1 [August 15, 1829]). Carlyle's hostile comments suggest the desirability of re-considering Professor Gerhart von Schulze-Gaevernitz's stress upon the resemblance between Comte's and Carlyle's views of the Reformation, the French Revolution, and the sceptical philosophers (see *Carlyle. Seine Welt- und Gesellschaftsanschauung,* pp. 116, 118, 128, 132). The resemblance is undeniable; but it probably derives from Comte's and Carlyle's indebtedness to a common source: the writings of Saint-Simon and of the Saint-Simonian Society.

[31] In *Frederick the Great,* Carlyle (in the person of " my Constitutional Historian ") alludes to sinful epochs: " '. . . sinful Epochs there are, when Heaven's curse has been spoken. . . .' " *History of Friedrich II of Prussia Called Frederick the Great* [London, Chapman and Hall, 1897-8], VI, 160). In " Cagliostro " (finished by March 21, 1833),

statements of the phoenix-doctrine of transition are lacking. With those three important parts formally lacking, whatever evidence there is of the influence of the Saint-Simonian concept of history upon *Frederick* lies in the tracing of periods in past history, in the prophecy of a new future period begun by the French Revolution, and in some elusive hints or implications of process. In *Frederick*, instead of using the term *periods*, Carlyle uses the term *acts* or *parts*. He designates three acts, or parts, in the drama of world-history. The French Revolution, he says,

is the New Act in World-History. New Act,—or, we may call it New *Part;* Drama of World-History, Part Third. If Part *Second* was 1,800 years ago, this I reckon will be Part *Third.* This is the truly celestial-infernal Event: the strangest we have seen for a thousand years. Celestial in one part; in the other, infernal. For it is withal the breaking-out of universal mankind into Anarchy, into the faith and practice of *No*-Government,—that is to say . . . , into unappeasable Revolt against Sham-Governors and Sham-Teachers,—which I do charitably define to be a Search, most unconscious, yet in deadly earnest, for true Governors and Teachers. That is the one fact of World-History worth dwelling on at this day. . . .[32]

Perhaps the unnamed First Act is classical Polytheistic Paganism; presumably the Second Act, begun in the early Christian times and ended by the French Revolution, is Catholic Feudalism; what the Third Act, begun by the French Revolution, will be is uncertain. But the designation of those three divisions, vague as it is,

Carlyle had used similar terminology. As before pointed out, the terminology in those two cases recalls the epoch of completed sinfulness in Fichte's *Die Grundzüge des Gegenwärtigen Zeitalters.* (See *Fichtes sämmtliche Werke,* VII, p. 12).

[32] *The History of Friedrich II of Prussia Called Frederick the Great,* VIII, 1-2.

recalls the much more specific divisions made by the Saint-Simonians.

The importance of the French Revolution he repeatedly stresses. After Frederick's twelve Herculean labors, the next marker in the history of mankind was the French Revolution, " That universal Burning-up, as in hell-fire, of Human Shams." [33] The great Frederick himself, with his labors, served to usher-in the greater event: " This also is one of the pecularities of Friedrich, that he is hitherto the last of the Kings; that he ushers-in the French Revolution, and closes an Epoch of World-History." [34] So complete was falsity in the Eighteenth Century that " the measure of the thing was full, and a French Revolution had to end it." And Carlyle adds that, for himself, that century has nothing grand in it "except that grand universal Suicide, named French Revolution, by which it terminated its otherwise most worthless existence. . . ." [35] Thus the French Revolution was, as he had long felt its immediate meaning to be, the negation of a negation, the Everlasting No; and in the long run it was the sweeper of the way for better things. Destroyer and preparer,—not quite preserver.

Nothwithstanding the anarchy of the present and the immediate future, Carlyle still retains a hope, a faith. But it is a hope deferred, until centuries of anarchy shall have abated:

Centuries of it yet lying ahead of us; several sad Centuries, sordidly tumultuous, and good for little! Say Two Centuries yet,—say even Ten of such a process: before the Old is completely burnt out, and the New in any state of sightliness? Millennium of Anarchies;—abridge it, spend your heart's-blood upon abridging it, ye Heroic Wise that are

[33] *Ibid.,* VIII, 1.   [34] *Ibid.,* I, 6.   [35] *Ibid.,* I, 8.

to come! For it is the consummation of All the Anarchies
that are and were;—which I do trust always means the
death (temporary death) of them! Death of the Anarchies:
or a world once more built wholly on Fact better or worse;
and the lying jargoning professor of Sham-Fact . . . becomes
a species extinct. . . . .[36]

Eventually, he believes, there will come again a social
organization, the principle and the details of which will
be credible.

Thus, though Carlyle's last great work lacks general discussion of the first three elements in the concept
of historical periodicity that we have been tracing, it
does contain, couched in dramatic terminology, a stipu-
lation of three Acts of world-history. Those three Acts
have the same broad dates as the three periods of the
Saint-Simonians. Two of those Acts, or periods, are in
the past, respectively before and after the First Century; the third, begun by the French Revolution, is to
be in the future. Carlyle again makes his familiar Ever-
lasting-No interpretation of the French Revolution, as
the ender of the old order and the clearer of the way
for the new. The new order that is ultimately to arise
in the future will be organized around a credible schema.
Thus much, it will probably be agreed, is mere restatement of Carlyle.

But here we approach dangerous ground. And the
next three sentences may be open to objection, as an
interpretation rather than a restatement. Underlying
Carlyle's faith as expressed in the passage concerning
the future of society, there may be still—though lightly
touched—some hints of the old concept of periodic
process, through alternate eras of faith and unfaith, by
means of phoenix transition. In his ejaculatory style

[36] *Ibid.,* VIII, 2.

Carlyle seems to mean that new credibilities and eras of belief follow old falsities and eras of unbelief. And when the old social body is burnt up, phoenix-fashion, the new will arise in a sightly condition.

After Carlyle finished the great work on Frederick, he still had a decade in which to write. However, he no longer discussed in his writings the concept of the historical process. Though he did not expound the law involved in that concept, he continued to interpret the contemporary results of the law. In his " Shooting Niagara: and After? " (1867),[37] in his " Early Kings of Norway " (1875),[38] and even in a late conversation with Allingham (1877),[39] he continued denouncing democracy and at the same time announcing its inevitability. And the denunciation of it as an evil simultaneously with the recognition of it as a necessity is the result of his concept of the historic process.

Unless one has followed step by step the progress of Carlyle's thought on history and his debt to the Saint-Simonians for his concept of historical periodicity, he will find little indisputable evidence of Saint-Simonian periodicity in the last four decades of Carlyle's life, from *Past and Present* on. The reason is Carlyle's shift in stress. As his phase of social prophecy develops, he no longer devotes large parts of his writing to exposition of the historical process, but simply assumes and implies the process as he discusses the last term of the process— the social conditions of the present and future. *Past and Present*, which contains the only reference to the Saint-Simonians during the 1840's, denounces, as Carlyle had frequently done before, the Society's religious

---

[37] *Essays*, V, 1. [38] *Essays*, V, 308.
[39] W. Allingham, *A Diary* (edited by H. Allingham and D. Radford, London, Macmillan, 1907), p. 261.

pretensions. Though this work of 1843 lacks the statement of the law of progressive periodic mutation and the statement of method of transition between periods, it contains some slight reflections of the Saint-Simonian philosophy of history. Perhaps the most notable now, merely because the most unusual, is Carlyle's use of the term *organic* to characterize the medieval Feudal Age and the future Industrial Age. If *Cromwell* shows anything of the Saint-Simonian concept, it does so by implication rather than by exposition. And the incidental comments in *Latter-Day Pamphlets* about the historical process are likewise hard to evaluate. So little exposition of the process is given that, except by recalling the writings of the 1830's and the steps in which Carlyle attained the prophet's mantle by converting the historian's robe, one could hardly pronounce definitely on Carlyle's debt to the Saint-Simonian concept. What seems to be the last published comment on the Saint-Simonians, in *Sterling,* 1851, is another condemnation of their religion—this time, of their religious fantasticalities and sectarianism. In the last of the great histories, *Frederick the Great* (published from 1858 to 1865), there is hardly as much generalizing as in even *Latter-Day Pamphlets* on the law of progressive periodic mutation and the method of transition between periods. But both law and method seem to me to be implied. And the figurative comments (in terms of dramatic acts) on the various periods in history are suggestive of the Saint-Simonian designation of periods. As was natural to his subject, the Eighteenth Century is greatly stressed: it is a preparation for the French Revolution. And the Revolution itself is the final negation of a negation, the Everlasting No in modern history, the clearer of the way for better things. In

Frederick, it seems to be Carlyle's concept of the historic process that, in spite of a most untoward present, gives him a hope of social regeneration. But that hope is in the far distant future, when, the old decayed order having been destroyed by anarchy and even the anarchy having passed away, new order will rise gradually out of ashes and disorder. In the final decade of his writing one finds less on the historic process than even the tenuous evidence shown from *Past and Present* through *Frederick*. But though he did not expound the process with its laws and principles and methods, he did continue until a few years before his death to interpret the result of the process. He continued denouncing democracy at the same time that he, in accordance with his philosophy of history, announced its inevitability. The utterances of the latter days, so often mistaken for mere fulminations of an irritable monster living out of his time, were in large part logically related developments of a systematic modern philosophy of history.

GENERAL SUMMARY

A summary statement of this whole study and its resulting conclusions may be helpful. We have attempted to examine carefully, because of its underlying importance and because of the inadequate treatment heretofore given it, the relation of Carlyle's concept of historical periodicity to the Saint-Simonian concept. Under the supposition that Carlyle might have developed his mature concept without the aid of the Saint-Simonians, we examined his early writings. In those early writings, before 1830, undoubtedly a concept of historical periodicity did exist. And from publication to publication, it was growing clearer. But up to August 1830, when Carlyle read his first Saint-Simonian documents, his concept lacked many characteristic features of the concept that occurs in the writings from 1831 to 1841. Of the various probable sources of the concept other than the Saint-Simonians, Goethe is the most striking. Unquestionably Goethe's notion of alternating epochs of *Glauben* and *Unglauben* made a powerful impression upon Carlyle's mind, and was an important and lasting influence on his works. But again, although the principle of alternating epochs is present in Goethe and Goethe makes some attempt to designate the occurrence of the epochs in actual past history, the Goethe concept falls short of Carlyle's mature concept in several important features.

We then turned to the ampler concept of historical periodicity found in the Saint-Simonian writings, and attempted to examine all available evidence bearing upon Carlyle's relations to that concept. The Saint-

Simonian concept, which includes the elements found in Goethe except his designation of a period in Hebrew history, contains five main elements. The French writings presenting the manifold expositions, elaborations, and implications of this five-fold concept came to Carlyle's attention in 1830 under conditions excellent for influencing his thought. During the year 1830-1831, according to his own statements, he read at least seven important works by Saint-Simon and by the Saint-Simonians. And he translated, and wrote an introduction for, the last of Saint-Simon's works. But he found himself more favorably impressed by the disciples than by the master. He commented upon finding well-expressed in the Saint-Simonian writings things that he had tried to say. Though from the first he looked askance at the Saint-Simonian religious views, he thought that their discussions on philosophy, morals, and politics carried their own conviction. He specifically pointed out, among the features that he especially approved, their delineation of the alternation of critical and organic epochs in human history. This same philosophy of history also especially struck John Stuart Mill and one or more individuals in the *Fraser's* group. And during Carlyle's early contact with those Londoners, at least Mill's high estimate probably cooperated with Carlyle's to make the impression permanent. But within a little over two years after Carlyle had first come to feel the importance of the moral, political, and philosophic thought of the Saint-Simonians, he condemned their religious tenets, believed their organization a failure, and considered their leader, Enfantin, a quack. Nevertheless, in spite of those facts, his works throughout the decade 1831—1841 show pronounced influence of the Saint-Simonian concept of periodicity.

During that decade, he fused the five Saint-Simonian elements with various elements of his own thought derived from other sources, and used all five elements thus fused—used most of them again and again—before 1841. The major works of that decade that show most marked influence are *Sartor*, "Characteristics," *The French Revolution, Lectures on the History of Literature,* and *Heroes.* But from *Past and Present* (1843) on, one becomes increasingly aware of a changed stress in Carlyle's writings. Elaborate expositions of the complete historic process no longer occur.

There is reason in the falling-off, from *Past and Present* on, in Carlyle's exposition of the process-part of the concept of historical periodicity. As the exposition of the process-part of the concept becomes almost negligible, the stress grows heavy upon social analysis of the present and upon social prophecy concerning the future. However, his philosophy of history had not changed. The last of the five elements in the Saint-Simonian concept of periodicity is the interpretation of the present and the future in the light of the law of progress through alternating epochs. That is, by *a posteriori* sociological methods of investigating past history, the historian discovers the laws of social change, becomes social philosopher, can analyze wisely present society, and can foretell the general nature—but not the details or the dates—of the future organization of society. Carlyle, following the elaborate Saint-Simonian philosophy of history and fusing it with his own insights and with other influences, had become convinced that the French Revolution marked the end of a whole historical period with its institutions and beliefs, and that the future era would have to work out institutions and beliefs capable of producing the unifying effect that had been produced in medieval times by Catholic Christianity and by Feudalism. From *Past and Present* through at least *Latter-Day Pamphlets* (though we have not here presented details of Carlyle's social philosophy), Carlyle became increasingly minute in his analysis of the condition of England, increasingly denunciatory of democracy, and increasingly positive and specific in his prescription for the future. And those strange denunciations of democracy, which were coupled with announcements of the necessity of democracy as a passing phase, continued on past his writing period, into the last years of his life. From *Sartor* on, the concept of the historic process, historical periodicity, as the Saint-Simonians had presented it underlies his social analysis and prophecy—interpreting the broad viewpoint, which we have given, and unifying many details, which we have not given. Carlyle became the social prophet that he did, because, in part at least, of the philosophy of history that he held.

A few more words may prevent misunderstanding concerning the kind of influence the Saint-Simonian concept of historical periodicity exerted upon Carlyle. It was the influence of a well-worked-out system upon a mind that had already moved a long way in the same direction but that had not yet clearly formulated and articulated its various insights and influences. The new influence stimulated and confirmed his insights into history and aided him in elaborating a reasonable scheme of historical change out of such dissimilar strains as the Eighteenth Century idea of progress and the Nineteenth Century historical method, his own Calvinistic belief in a world-order that was God's will and the unCalvinistic Goethe's notion of alternating epochs of belief and unbelief. The Saint-Simonians' systematic concept of periodicity was inclusive enough to interpret satisfactorily to Carlyle, not only the vast historic process in the past, but also, as part of that continuing process, his own *milieu*. In that philosophy of history, classical religions and polities, Catholicism and feudalism, protestantism, the Eighteenth Century, the French Revolution, democracy, and the manifold social confusions of his own time had their places and became intelligible parts of a whole. This concept of historic periodicity enabled him to state with considerable definiteness a law acting underneath the phenomena of the past and present and adumbrating the phenomena of the future. And from that high vantage point he pronounced with Hebraic sternness the wrath to come upon those men and nations, past and present, that failed to adjust to the unchanging law.

BIBLIOGRAPHY

Allingham, William, *A Diary* (ed. by H. Allingham and D. Radford), London, Macmillian, 1907.
Barrault, E., *Aux Artistes. Du passé et de l'avenir des beaux-arts,* Paris, 1830. (This pamphlet of about 80 pages is unsigned. Duke University owns a copy, which, with a number of other pamphlets, is bound up under the title *Religion Saint-Simonienne. Réunion générale*).
Booth, A. J., *Saint-Simon and Saint-Simonism,* London, Longmans, Green, Reader, and Dyer, 1871.
Carlyle, Jane Welsh, *Early Letters of Jane Welsh Carlyle Together with a Few of Later Years and Some of Thomas Carlyle* (ed. by David G. Ritchie), London, Swan Sonnenschein and Company, 1889.
Carlyle, Thomas, *The Letters of Thomas Carlyle, 1826-1836* (ed. C. E. Norton), London, 1889.
——, *Two Note Books of Thomas Carlyle* (ed. C. E. Norton), Grolier Club, New York, 1898.
——, *Briefe Thomas Carlyle's an Varnhagen von Ense aus den Jahren 1837-1857* (tr. and ed. by Richard Preuss), Berlin, Paetel, 1892.
——, *Lettres de Thomas Carlyle à sa mère* (tr. and ed. by E. Masson), Paris, 1907.
——, " Carlyle's Letters to the Socialists of 1830," *The New Quarterly* (London), II (1909), 277-288. (See also under D'Eichthal, E.).
——, *Letters of Thomas Carlyle to John Stuart Mill, John Sterling and Robert Browning* (ed. by A. Carlyle), London, Unwin, 1923.
——, *German Romance. Translations from the German* (Centenary edition), London, Chapman and Hall, 1898.
——, *Wilhelm Meister's Apprenticeship and Travels, Translated from the German of Goethe* (Centenary edition), London, Chapman and Hall, 1899.
——, *Critical and Miscellaneous Essays,* 5 volumes (Centenary edition), London, Chapman and Hall, 1899.
——, *Sartor Resartus* (ed. C. F. Harrold), New York, Doubleday, Doran and Company, 1937.
——, *The French Revolution. A History* (Centenary edition), London, Chapman and Hall, 1898.
——, *Lectures on the History of Literature, or The Successive Periods of European Culture* (ed. R. P. Karkaria), London, Curwen, Kane and Co., 1892. (Karkaria edited Anstey's original manuscript-report of Carlyle's lectures of 1838. J. R. Greene in the same year edited (in American and then in English editions) a copy of Anstey's manuscript).
——, *On Heroes, Hero-Worship and the Heroic in History* (Centenary edition), London, Chapman and Hall, 1901.
——, *Past and Present* (Centenary edition), London, Chapman and Hall, 1897.

Carlyle, Thomas, *Oliver Cromwell's Letters and Speeches, with Elucida-tions* (Centenary edition), London, Chapman and Hall, 1897.

——, *Latter-Day Pamphlets* (Centenary edition), London, Chapman and Hall, 1898.

——, *The Life of John Sterling* (Centenary edition), London, Chapman and Hall, 1897.

——, *History of Friedrich II of Prussia Called Frederick the Great* (Centenary edition), London, Chapman and Hall, 1897-1898. Eight volumes.

——, *History of German Literature*, Volume I. (This unpublished autograph manuscript, formerly in the possession of the late Alexander Carlyle and sold by Sotheby in 1932, is now in the Manuscript Vault of Yale University Library. Only this Volume I, consisting of 90 pages (pp. 1-68 and 89-110), is known to exist. The missing twenty pages (pp. 69-88) of the original 110 were taken out early in 1831 by Carlyle and re-worked for publication in the form of essays. Although on August 31, 1830, Carlyle told Goethe (*Correspondence between Goethe and Carlyle*, pp. 209-210) that he had written a volume and a half of the projected four volumes of the *History* and had thus brought his narrative down to the Reformation, the fragment of the second volume has dis-appeared. The present Volume I, which deals with German literature through the Swabian Era, was finished late in May or early in June 1830 (see *Letters of Thomas Carlyle, 1826-1836*, p. 164, and *Two Note Books*, p. 156). Carlyle's late entries (August and September 1866) on the last page of the manuscript erroneously date it 1829 and show some other evidences of con-fusion only natural a whole generation after the work had been suspended and laid aside).

——, "*Industrial Regiments.*" (This unpublished autograph manu-script, formerly in the possession of the late Alexander Carlyle and sold by Sotheby in 1932, is now in the Manuscript Vault of the Yale University Library. The manuscript consists of thirteen sheets, each sheet numbered on only the front side but written on both sides, making twenty-six pages in all. At the upper left corner of p. 1, there are written in Carlyle's hand the words "Industrial reg^ts: consider it better." The unnumbered side of the seventh sheet bears evidence valuable in determining the date of composition: "Yesternight (15 Novr 1848). . . ." This writing attempts to solve the Irish problem by converting the idle laborers into industrial regiments and putting them to self-sustaining public works such as the reclaiming of waste lands. Thus it is related to parts of the *Latter-Day Pamphlets* of 1850.)

Carlyle, Thomas and Emerson, R. W., *Correspondence of Carlyle and Emerson, 1834-1872* (ed. by C. E. Norton), Boston, Osgood, 1883.

Carlyle, Thomas and Goethe, J. W. von, *Correspondence between Goethe and Carlyle* (ed. C. E. Norton), London, 1887.

Cazamian, Louis, *Carlyle* (Les Grands Écrivains Étrangers), Paris, Bloud et cie, 1913.

Cofer, D. B., *Saint-Simonism in the Radicalism of Thomas Carlyle*, College Station, Texas, 1931.

Coleridge, S. T., *The Works of Samuel Taylor Coleridge*, Philadelphia, Crissy and Markley, 1849.

————, *Aids to Reflection* (ed. by H. N. Coleridge; with Preliminary Essay by John M'Vickor; sixth edition, revised and corrected), New York, Stanford and Swords, 1847.

————, *Essays and Lectures on Shakspeare and Some Other Old Poets and Dramatists* (Everyman's Library edition), London, J. M. Dent and Sons, 1907.

Dunoyer, B. C., " Esquisse historique des doctrines auxquelles on a donné le nom d'*Industrialisme*, c'est-à-dire, des doctrines qui fondent la société sur l'*Industrie*," *Revue encyclopédique*, XXXIII (February, 1827), 368-394.

Eckermann, Johann Peter, *Gespräche mit Goethe in den letzten Jahren seines Lebens* (Herausgegeben von Conrad Höfer), Leipzig, Hesse und Becker Verlag, 1913.

D'Eichthal, Eugène, " Carlyle et la Saint-Simonisme," *La Revue historique*, LXXXII (1903), 292-306.

Enfantin, P. See Saint-Simon et Enfantin.

Fichte, J. G., *Fichte's sämmtliche Werke* (ed. J. H. Fichte), Leipzig, 1845.

[*Fraser's* Group], " Letter on the Doctrine of St. Simon," *Fraser's Magazine*, V (July, 1832), 666-669.

————, " Oliver Yorke at Home. No. III. A Dialogue with Johann Wolfgang von Goethe," *Fraser's Magazine*, V (February, 1832), 22-34.

Froude, J. A., *Thomas Carlyle: A History of the First Forty Years of His Life: 1795-1835*, New York, Scribner's, 1882.

————, *Thomas Carlyle: A History of His Life in London: 1834-1881*, London, Longmans, Green and Company, 1919.

Goethe, J. W. von, *Sämmtliche Werke* (ed. K. Goedeke), Stuttgart, n. d.

Griggs, E. L., " *The Friend*: 1809 and 1818 Editions," *Modern Philology*, XXXV (May 1938), 369-373.

Halévy, E., *A History of the English People*, London, 1927. (Original French edition 1912).

Harrold, C. F., *Carlyle and German Thought: 1819-1834* (*Yale Studies in English*, LXXXII), New Haven, Yale University Press, 1934.

Hunt, H. J., *Le Socialisme et le romantisme en France: Etude de la presse socialiste de 1830 à 1848*, Oxford, Clarendon Press, 1935.

Lehman, B. H., *Carlyle's Theory of the Hero: Its Sources, Development, History, and Influence on Carlyle's Work. A Study of a Nineteenth Century Idea*, Durham, Duke University Press, 1928.

Lessing, G. E., *L'Education du genre humain, par Lessing, traduit, pour la première fois, de l'Allemand, par Eugène Rodiques*, Paris, 1832 (Original Paris edition, 1829).

Mill, J. S., *Autobiography* (ed. J. J. Coss), New York, 1924.
————, *Correspondence inédite avec Gustave d'Eichthal* (ed. by Eugène d'Eichthal), Paris, 1898.
————, *The Letters of John Stuart Mill* (ed. by H. S. R. Elliot), London, 1910.
Murphy, Ella, M., " Carlyle and the Saint-Simonians," *Studies in Philology*, XXXIII (January 1936), 93-118.
Napier, Macvey, *Selection from the Correspondence of the Late Macvey Napier, Esq.* (ed. by his son, Macvey Napier), London, Macmillan, 1879.
Neff, Emery, *Carlyle and Mill.* An Introduction to Victorian Thought. Second revised edition, New York, Columbia University Press, 1926.
————, *Carlyle*, New York, 1932.
Potter, G. R., " Coleridge and the Idea of Evolution," *P M L A*, XL (1925), 379-397.
Saint-Simon, C. H. de R., *Nouveau Christianisme*, Paris, 1832. (Original edition, Paris, 1825).
Saint-Simon, C. H. de R. and others, *L'Industrie. Ou Discussions politiques, morales et philosophiques,* 4 volumes, Paris, 1817-1818. Actually, large and important parts of this work were signed by Saint-Aubin, A. Thierry, J. A. Chaptal, and some author who used the mere initial " M***." For some material reprinted from *L'Industrie*, see *Oeuvres de Saint-Simon et d'Enfantin*, Vol. XIX.
Saint-Simon, C. H. de R., et Enfantin, Prosper, *Œuvres de Saint-Simon et d'Enfantin.* Publiées par les membres du conseil institué par Enfantin pour l'éxécution de ses dernières voluntés, Paris, 1865-1878, 47 volumes.
Saint-Simonian Society, *Le Producteur, Journal de l'industrie, des sciences et des beaux-arts*, Paris, 1825-1826, 5 volumes. (At first a weekly; beginning with May 1, 1826, it became a monthly).
————, *L'Organisateur, Journal des progrés de la science générale*, Paris, August 15, 1829-August 15, 1831. (A weekly periodical averaging, during its last year, some eight pages to the issue. On April 18, 1830, it adopted the subtitle *Journal de la doctrine de Saint-Simon.* This periodical should not be confused with *L'Organisateur* of 1819.
————, *Le Globe*, Paris, 1830-1832. (This periodical, begun in Paris Sept. 15, 1824, and published on alternate days with the subtitle *Journal Philosophique et littéraire*, had changed to daily publication before it became a Saint-Simonian organ on November 11, 1830. On January 18, 1831, the subtitle changed to *Journal de la doctrine de Saint-Simon.* On January 1, 1832, the subtitle again changed to *Journal de la religion de Saint-Simonienne.* On April 20, 1832, it ceased publication).
————, *Doctrine de Saint-Simon, Exposé première année, 1829* (ed. C. Bouglé and Elie Halévy), Paris, 1924. (The first edition appeared in Paris, August 1830.)

Saint-Simonian Society, *Exposition de la doctrine Saint-Simonienne. Deuxième année.* Originally published in Paris, December, 1830; republished, Paris, 1877, in Vol. XLII of the 47-volume *Œuvres de Saint-Simon et d'Enfantin.* (Ten of the thirteen lectures that constitute this Exposition, 2nd year, were published in the weekly *L'Organisateur* between December 20, 1829, and July 13, 1830. The three omitted from *L'Organisateur* are Lectures VI, VII and IX).

————, *Religion Saint-Simonienne,* Paris, 1831.

————, *Procès en la cour d'assises de la Seine, les 27 et 28 aôut 1832,* Paris, 1832. (This 405-page book has, as its general title, *Religion Saint-Simonienne.* This *procès* is also included in Vol. XLVII of *Œuvres de Saint-Simon et d'Enfantin,* Paris, 1878. The last few pages give important information concerning the dates and quantities of works published by the Society.)

————, *Procès en Police correctionnelle, le 19 octobre 1832,* Paris, 1832. (This 105-page book has, as its general title, *Religion Saint-Simonienne.* This Procès is also included in Vol. XLVII of *Œuvres de Saint-Simon et d'Enfantin,* Paris, 1878).

Schanck, Nikolaus, " Die Sozial-Politischen Anschauungen Coleridges und sein Einfluss auf Carlyle," *Bonner Studien zur Englischen Philologie,* Hft. 16 (1924).

Schlegel, Friedrich von, *Friedrich von Schlegels sämmtliche Werke,* Wien, 1846.

————, *Lectures on the History of Literature, Ancient and Modern* (tr. H. G. Bohn), London, G. Bell and Sons, 1896.

Schulze-Gaevernitz, Gerhart von, *Carlyle. Seine Welt- und Gesellschaftsanschauung* (second ed.), Halle, 1897.

Shepherd, R. H., *Memoirs of the Life and Writings of Thomas Carlyle,* London, W. H. Allen and Company, 1881.

Shine, Hill, " Carlyle and the German Philosophy Problem During the Year 1826-1827," *P M L A,* L (1935), 807-827.

————, " Carlyle and *Fraser's* ' Letter on the Doctrine of St. Simon,' " *Notes and Queries,* CLXXI (1936), 290-293.

————, *Carlyle's Fusion of Poetry, History, and Religion by 1834,* Chapel Hill, University of North Carolina Press, 1938.

Southey, Robert, " Doctrine de Saint-Simon. Exposition. Première Année," *The Quarterly Review,* XLV (No. 90, July 1831), 407-450.

Taylor, A. C., *Carlyle et la pensée latine (Etudes de littérature étrangère et comparée, 8),* Paris, Boivin, 1937.

Tuell, Anne Kimball, " Carlyle's Marginalia in Sterling's *Essays and Tales,*" *P M L A,* LIV (September, 1939), 815-824.

Wilson, D. A., *Carlyle to " The French Revolution,"* London, 1924.

————, *Carlyle at His Zenith, 1848-1853,* London, 1927.

Young, Louise Merwin, *Thomas Carlyle and the Art of History,* Philadelphia, University of Pennsylvania Press, 1939.

INDEX

(The chronological order used in the text for the discussion of Carlyle's individual writings makes reference to them unnecessary in this index. But since the works of the Saint-Simonians are not so readily located in the text, they are listed here in alphabetical order, under *Saint-Simon* and under *Saint-Simonian Society Publications.*)

187